ALL IS ONE

ALL IS ONE

A COMMENTARY ON
SRI VAIYAI R. SUBRAMANIAN'S
ELLAM ONDRE

BY

ABBOT GEORGE BURKE
(SWAMI NIRMALANANDA GIRI)

*If you want moksha, read and practice
the instructions in Ellam Ondre.*
(Ramana Maharshi)

LIGHT OF THE SPIRIT
PRESS
CEDAR CREST, NEW MEXICO

Published by
Light of the Spirit Press
lightofthespiritpress.com

Light of the Spirit Monastery
P. O. Box 1370
Cedar Crest, New Mexico 87008
OCOY.org

ISBN-13: 978-1-955046-11-4

Library of Congress Control Number: 2022940956

Bisac categories:
1. REL032030 RELIGION / Hinduism / Sacred Writings
2. OCC010000 BODY, MIND & SPIRIT / Mindfulness & Meditation
3. REL062000 RELIGION / Spirituality

1st edition
06292022

Cover: The Arunachaleshwar Temple in Tiruvannamalai, photographed
from the slopes of the holy mountain of Arunachala in Tamil Nadu, India

Dedicated to Renaat and Denise Vermeir
Friends and Fellow Sadhakas

Contents

INTRODUCTION

"This is the knowledge above all other: purifier and king of secrets, only made plain to the eye of the mystic. Great is its virtue, its practice easy: thus man is brought to truth eternal" (Bhagavad Gita 9:2).

Ellam Ondre was written in the nineteenth century in Tamil. It became widely known by the frequent recommendation of Sri Ramana Maharshi. (The chapter titles were added by him.) Its great value lies in the fact that it does not just speak of principles of the highest Advaitic philosophy, but also includes practical advice on cultivating and becoming established in the non-dual state of consciousness that is liberation. It offers clarity instead of clichés.

When I sent a copy of it by email to my friends Renaat and Denise Vermier, Renaat immediately replied saying that they needed a commentary on it. So here it is.

Abbot George Burke
(Swami Nirmalananda Giri)

PREFACE OF THE AUTHOR OF *ELLAM ONDRE*

Men court happiness and shun misery. It is the same with other beings also. This holds good for the common run of mankind. But the higher order is bent upon right conduct, enduring patiently the good or evil that it may bring. Fellowship with these will be lasting, whereas fellowship with ordinary people will not be. Good will result to the world through fellowship with the higher order only.

The question then arises: "What is right?" The point is important, but the answer has not been found. Why? Because what is right is determined by circumstances. However comprehensive a work may be written on the subject, there will always be circumstances not envisaged by the author. Therefore it becomes necessary to realize that state which will enable us to assess the various conditions and determine what is right.

That state is one only. There are no states like it. Although it is single, it is extraordinary that the worldly wise consider it exceedingly rare. Nothing can be more extraordinary than this. That unique state is very clearly taught in the Upanishads. In this book I have put down the same truth according to my understanding. I have considered it my duty. I do not claim originality. The six chapters of this book are so closely interrelated that some point which may be expected in one chapter may be found in another. Again a few points which may not be clear on a superficial reading will become clear upon closer study. More may be gathered from major works or Sages.

Universal Mother, Master true, save us!

The Author

CHAPTER ONE–UNITY

1. All, including the world seen by you and yourself, the seer of the world, is one only.

2. All that you consider as I, you, he, she and it, is one only.

3. What you consider to be sentient beings and what you consider to be insentient, such as earth, air, fire and water is all one.

4. The good which is derived by your considering all as one cannot be had by considering each as separate from the other. Therefore all is one.

5. The knowledge of the unity of all is good for you and good for others as well. Therefore all is one.

6. He who sees "I am separate," "you are separate," "he is separate" and so on, acts one way to himself and another way to others. He cannot help doing so. The thought "I am separate, others are separate" is the seed from which grows the tree of differing actions in relation to different persons. How can there be any lapse from righteousness for a person who knows the unity of himself with others? As long as the germ of differentiation is there, the tree of differing actions will flourish, even unawares. Therefore give up differentiation. All is one only.

7. Ask: "If in the world all things appear different, how can I consider all as one? Is there any way of gaining this knowledge?" The reply is: "In the same tree we see leaves, flowers, berries

and branches, different from one another, yet they are all one because they are all included in the word 'tree.' Their root is the same; their sap is the same. Similarly, all things, all bodies, all organisms are from the same source and activated by a single life principle." Therefore all is one.

8. Oh good man! Is the statement that "All is one" good or evil? Think for yourself. Just as the person will always be righteous who regards himself like others and others like himself, how can any evil attach itself to him who knows himself to be others and the others to be himself? Tell me if there is any better way for obtaining good than the knowledge of unity? Certainly other methods cannot be as good as this one. How can anyone love others more than when knowing them to be himself, to know them in unity–love as unity, for they are truly one.

9. Who can share the mental peace and freshness of the knower of unity? He has no cares. The Good of all is his own good. A mother considers her children's well-being to be her own well-being. Still, her love is not perfect because she thinks she is separate and her children are separate. The love of a Sage, who has realized the unity of all, far excels even the love of a mother. There is no other means of gaining such love than the knowledge of unity. Therefore all is one.

10. Know that the world as a whole is your undecaying body and that you are the everlasting life of the whole world. Tell me if there is any harm in doing so. Who fears to go the harmless way? Be courageous. The Vedas teach this very truth. There is nothing but yourself. All good will be yours. Yea, you become the good itself. All that others gain from you will be good only.

Who will work evil to his own body and soul? A remedy is applied if there is an abscess in the body. Even if the remedy is painful, it is meant to do good only. Such will be some of your actions; they will also be for the good of the world. For that reason, you will not be involved in differentiation. I put it briefly: The knower of unity will act as one should. In fact, the knowledge of unity makes him act. He cannot err. In the world, he is God made visible.

All is one.

Commentary

We approach any experience or idea with preconceptions, with a frame of reference that is habitual with us. This small book is about Unity on various levels. It is necessary for us to realize that this first chapter is about the individual and his relationship with the phenomenal world and those living with him in that world. If we begin to read while holding the idea of the absolute unity of Brahman with all that seems to be Its "else" the words will appear to be nonsense. Or we will reduce them to nonsense ourselves by our refusal to look at the words as they are, insisting on bending them into the context of the highest Advaita teaching. But this chapter begins and ends with the practical view of the world and its human inhabitants. That is all.

For the last nineteen years of her life on this earth I was closely associated with Anandamayi Ma. Those who encountered Ma, whether her devotees or not, naturally tried to define her, for that is how human beings normally gain understanding. But

Ma was truly Something Other, and often in people's questioning of her in an effort to fit her into a context or definition would adamantly say: "Leave this body out of it!" (Ma usually referred to herself as "this body.") The same is true in this first chapter: Leave Brahman and its absolute nature out of the matter. This is just about us as individual evolving consciousnesses and our relation to the world around us and the people in it. The rest will come later.

   1. All, including the world seen by you and yourself, the seer of the world, is one only.

   Not only is Brahman absolutely One, so is the entire relative world and all within it, for only oneness can be projected ("created") by the One. Otherwise It would violate Its own nature–which is an impossibility. The author says "you and yourself" to indicate that the world is seen by our bodily senses and that stimulus is relayed to our brain which in turn is relayed to the senses of our subtle bodies which in turn relay that to our consciousness, who is the seer. When Sri Ramakrishna was asked, "What is the Self," he replied: "The witness of the mind," the mind being the complex comprised of the subtle bodies. And in reality the seen, the seeing and the seer are really one.

   It is essential to understand that the word "one" can mean more than a single concept. In our simplistic (lazy) way of thinking we assume it means only a number, but one is a quality, a condition, as well. You cannot speak of the Divine Unity as you would of a single egg–this is the continual error Western thinking, and sad to say some in India (perhaps educated in the Western manner) do the same. Always we must remember that Advaita does not mean One. It only means Not Two. So Monism is a profound error, even through in East and West many think it is Advaita.

If this sounds like mere word juggling, it is because we do not have the perspective of yogis—the only people who really understand the truth of Advaita which is transcendent and therefore completely beyond the limited intellect of anyone. Ultimately Advaita is a state of being, the state of true vidya, of true knowing, that is itself moksha: total liberation and enlightenment.

Notice that the author begins his statement: "All, including the world," implying that there is much, much more to the All That Is than just us, our perceptions and anything we perceive. Regarding that All, the Kena Upanishad (2.3) says: "To whomsoever It [Brahman] is not known, to him It is known: to whomsoever It is known, he does not know. It is not understood by those who understand It; it is understood by those who do not understand it." The interpretive translation by Swami Prabhavananda make this more clear: "He truly knows Brahman who knows him as beyond knowledge; he who thinks that he knows, knows not. The ignorant think that Brahman is known, but the wise know him to be beyond knowledge."

2. All that you consider as I, you, he, she and it, is one only.

Again, please realize that he does not mean this in relation to Brahman. Later the author will be speaking of the highest truth that Brahman is truly *Ekam Evam Advityam*, One, Only, Without a Second, but here he is introducing us to the idea that we are one with all the human beings we encounter in our life. His intention is that we should understand that we are all one in essence, part of the One Life. We are all waves on the ocean of divine manifestation, all rooted in the divine, but none of us are the totality of the divine.

I emphasize this because there are books of Advaitic philosophy that would make us believe that when we attain the ultimate enlightenment we will say: "I am everything" and we will not longer perceive anything else. What an awful thing it would be to come to the end of the evolutionary road and find that there was nothing left but "me"!

At this point the author is not speaking of Brahman at all, only of the way we view ourselves and others–a view that of course must be in the perspective of the Reality that is Brahman.

3. What you consider to be sentient beings and what you consider to be insentient, such as earth, air, fire and water is all one.

4. The good which is derived by your considering all as one cannot be had by considering each as separate from the other. Therefore all is one.

5. The knowledge of the unity of all, is good for you and good for others as well. Therefore all is one.

6. He who sees "I am separate," "you are separate," "he is separate" and so on, acts one way to himself and another way to others. He cannot help doing so. The thought "I am separate, others are separate" is the seed from which grows the tree of differing actions in relation to different persons. How can there be any lapse from righteousness for a person who knows the unity of himself with others? As long as the germ of differentiation is there, the tree of differing actions will flourish, even unawares. Therefore give up differentiation. All is one only.

Those who see this separation of others from themselves act accordingly, making a non-existent differentiation. This denies the two wisdom statements of Jesus: "All things whatsoever ye would that men should do to you, do ye even so to them" (Matthew 7:12). "Inasmuch as ye have done it unto one of the least of these my brethren, ye have done it unto me" (Matthew 25:40). In this second statement we see that Jesus considered himself at one with all men, that what we do to anyone we do to ourselves and ultimately to all humanity. It is like dropping a stone into a pond whose waves move throughout the entire body of water and affect it. Those who see this as true will not relapse from righteous thought and behavior regarding his fellow human beings.

Writing this I can see and hear after sixty-three years dear Brother Crawley talking at a gathering of our church one Christmastide. The church I belonged to was begun in 1880, and from the first day taught the unity of all human beings and actively opposed racial segregation, establishing fully integrated churches. Naturally, for years the Klan did all it could to destroy the little church (they failed), and even in the 1950s burned down our church building in Pasadena, which was right next to Alhambra where the American Nazi Party had its headquarters.

Brother Crawley was from Alabama, and he said in his talk that he had told some other black people, "I am going up to Guthrie [Oklahoma]. We are all one up there and love each other and worship together as brothers and sisters." "But that's against the law," objected one of those he was speaking to. "We don't care," Brother Crawley told him, "We do it anyway!" The next summer one of our ministers told me that he had gone to pick up Brother Crawley in Missouri for a church meeting there. "When Brother Crawley got off the bus we hugged and kissed each other, and I thought the woman who ran the bus station was going to have a heart attack," he told me. But, as Brother Crawley said, we did it anyway. A few years later a friend and I were stopped by the police in Hollywood and falsely given a jaywalking ticket. Four other people had walked across the street at the same time during the green light, but the police said we two had walked across at a red light. Why? My friend was black. I'm glad "we did it anyway."

7. Ask: *"If in the world all things appear different, how can I consider all as one? Is there any way of gaining this knowledge?"* The reply is: *"In the same tree we see leaves, flowers, berries and branches, different from one another, yet they are all one because they are all included in the word 'tree.' Their root is the same; their sap is the same. Similarly, all things, all bodies, all organisms are from the same source and activated by a single life principle."* Therefore all is one.

This is the practical perspective we must have of ourselves and all humanity. Anyone can say, "It is all one," but we must be those who live it.

This verse makes me think of my beloved Aunt Faye, who was father, mother and spiritual teacher to me from my age of six. During World War II she had gone to the south to be near my uncle George who was a patient in a military hospital. To manage this financially she got a job in Little Rock at Ottenheimer's dress factory. Quite a few black people worked there at the lowest level jobs and wages, and Aunt Faye became friends with several of them. They used to come and tell her when they were being pushed around or mistreated by the supervisors, and she would go and complain and get them to stop. They also told her a lot of their griefs that took place outside the factory. She would tell me about them and literally cry bitter tears and say, "I am so worried about my friends because they don't have anyone to speak up for them."

Her bitterest memory was when one of the black workers came to her and asked to speak to her alone. He then asked her if she thought God had cursed the black people and made them that color. (This was and is common teaching in some churches. Supposedly the black people are descendants of Ham, the son of Noah whom Noah cursed and said his descendants would be slaves. See Genesis 9:22-27. One of my black friends from the island of Saint Thomas told me that she was taught this by black teachers when she went to school.)

"When he asked me that," Aunt Faye told me, "I called inside to God to help me answer him." And she began to point out to him that in all the things God created he made many differences, that every species of living being had many shapes and sizes and especially colors. And so it was with human beings that were all equal but different in appearance, and she quoted to him, "God that made the world and all things therein, hath made of one blood all nations of men for to dwell on all the face of the earth" (Acts 7:24, 26). Her friend smiled and said, "Yes, that's right; that's right!" and went away smiling. "But I," Aunt Faye told me, "ran behind the bales of dress goods and cried and cried, just thinking of how terrible and cruel it was that anyone would tell my friends that God through Noah had cursed them and wanted them to be nothing but slaves and servants." She had not read *Ellam Ondre*, but she had the same understanding.

8. *Oh good man! Is the statement that "All is one" good or evil? Think for yourself. Just as the person will always be righteous who regards himself like others and others like himself, how can any evil attach itself to him who knows himself to be others and the others to be himself? Tell me if there is any better way for obtaining good than the knowledge of unity? Certainly other methods cannot be as good as this one. How can anyone love others more than when knowing them to be himself, to know them in unity–love as unity, for they are truly one.*

There really is no need for commentary on this, but I wanted it to be presented here on its own in order to emphasize the divine truth of this verse and the divine wisdom of embodying its ideals in our own individual lives.

9. *Who can share the mental peace and freshness of the knower of unity? He has no cares. The Good of all is his own good. A mother considers her children's well-being to be her own well-being. Still, her love is not perfect because she thinks she is separate and her children are separate. The love of a Sage, who has realized the unity of all, far excels even the love of a mother. There is no other means of*

gaining such love than the knowledge of unity. Therefore all is one.
This is truly divinely inspired wisdom. Certainly in Swami Sivananda of Rishikesh I saw this lived out daily. He lived in perfect consciousness of The One and therefore saw It in us. By this he inspired us with faith in our own true selves and the possibility of realizing It just as fully as had Sivanandaji. He signed all his letters: "Thine Own Self." In him was embodied the truth of the saying:

> The parents give birth,
> But the guru gives life.
> There is an end to birth,
> But there is no end to life.

10. Know that the world as a whole is your undecaying body and that you are the everlasting life of the whole world. Tell me if there is any harm in doing so. Who fears to go the harmless way? Be courageous. The Vedas teach this very truth. There is nothing but yourself. All good will be yours. Yea, you become the good itself. All that others gain from you will be good only. Who will work evil to his own body and soul? A remedy is applied if there is an abscess in the body. Even if the remedy is painful, it is meant to do good only. Such will be some of your actions; they will also be for the good of the world. For that reason, you will not be involved in differentiation. I put it briefly: The knower of unity will act as one should. In fact, the knowledge of unity makes him act. He cannot err. In the world, he is God made visible.
All is one.

The "you" that is "the everlasting life of the whole world" is your true Self, the jivatman that is one with the Universal Self, the Paramatman, that is *in* all things and *is* all things. But since there is no essential difference between one jivatman and another, is it reasonable for someone to conclude "I am the everlasting life of the whole world" alone? If all jivas are one, cannot they all make the same claim if they see things as I do?

So we see the folly of identifying our little false and ignorant "I" with the Infinite "I" that is all things. Without true Self-realization we dare not say, "I am That." This would be the illusion of the satanic ego–total spiritual insanity. Rather the truth is: THAT Am I. THAT comes first, I comes second. That is the whole and I am the part. That is why the sadhana mantra is Soham (That Am I: pronounced "Sohum") and not Hamsa (I Am That). (See *Soham Yoga: The Yoga of the Self.*) We have to get our ideas in the right order. Otherwise philosophically we will be putting the cart before the horse.

Now see how the author asks, "Who fears to go the harmless way?" Ahimsa is not just the resolve to injure no one, it is also the insight into the unity of all being, of existence itself. If an insight is not lived out consistently in the life of a sadhaka, then that insight is, practically speaking a mirage, not a reality. We must make these sublime insights of the ancient sages of India a living reality in our life, whatever others might choose (or fail) to do. And to embark on that resolve does indeed require great, even superhuman, courage. But since we are not merely human, it is possible for us to do so. Sri Ramakrishna said, "When Shiva realizes His own Self, He dances about in joy exclaiming, 'What am I! What am I!'" We, like Shiva, must awaken and rejoice, saying, "O! What I am! What I am!" But there are countless ones who should be doing the same. We will not be alone with a tiny, satisfied ego. So we will see that they, too, are "God made visible." For truly: All is one.

CHAPTER TWO–YOU

1. Who are you? Are you this body? If so, why are you not aware of a serpent crawling on it when you are in deep sleep? So then can you be this body? No, certainly not. You must be other than this body.

2. Sometimes in sleep you dream. There you identify yourself with someone. Can you be that one? You cannot be. Otherwise, what becomes of that individual on your waking? You are not he. Furthermore, you are ashamed of having identified yourself with him. Clearly, you are not that particular person. You are the one that stands apart from him.

3. Recall the state of dreamless slumber. What is your state then? Can that be your true nature? Surely you will not subscribe to this belief. Why? Because you are not so foolish as to identify yourself with the massive darkness which obstructs you from knowing the state you are in. Discerned by the intellect from the things around, how can you admit yourself to be the same as ignorance or blank? Or, how can it truly be your real nature? It cannot be. You are the knower who knows that this state remains one of dense darkness veiling your true nature. How can you be that which you have experienced and condemned? Therefore you are not the dark ignorance of deep sleep. You stand apart from this too.

4. When it is said that even this gross body is not you, can you be any other thing which is yet farther away from you? In the same way that you are not this gross body, you are not anything farther from the body, nor the dream person, nor the ignorance of deep sleep. You are distinct from these three states and this world.

5. These three states can be reduced to two conditions only—namely, the one of the subject and object, and the other is the unawareness of the subject itself. The former includes the waking and dream states, whereas the latter represents deep slumber. All your experiences are comprised in these two conditions only. Both of them are foreign to you. Your true nature remains distinct from them.

6. If you ask what that is, it is called turiya, which means the fourth state. Why is this name used? This name is proper because it seems to say the three states of your experience—waking, dream and deep sleep—are foreign to you and your true state is the fourth, which is different from these three. Should the three states, waking, dream and deep sleep, be taken to form one long dream, the fourth state represents the waking from this dream. Thus it is more withdrawn than deep sleep, also more wakeful than the waking state. Therefore your true state is that fourth one which is distinguished from the waking, dream and deep sleep states. You are that only.

7. What is this fourth state? It is knowledge which does not particularize anything. It is not unaware of itself. That is to say, the fourth state is Pure Knowledge which is not conscious of any object, but not unconscious itself. Only he who

has realized it even for a trice, has realized the Truth. You are that only.

8. What is there more for him who has gained the fourth state? Practically, it is not possible for anyone to remain forever in that state, that is, the state of no particular knowledge. He who has realized the fourth state later wakes up in this world, but for him this world is not as before. He sees that what he realized as the fourth state shines forth as all this. He will not imagine this world as distinct from that Pure Knowledge. Thus what he saw within, he now sees without in a different form. In the place of the differentiation of old, he is now established in the state of non-differentiation everywhere. Now, he is all. There is nothing distinct from himself. His eyes closed or open, howsoever the things may change, his state remains unchanged. This is the state of Brahman. This is the natural eternal state. You are that ever-true state.

9. There is nothing beyond this state. The words, "inward" and "outward" have no meaning for him. All is one. His body, speech and mind cannot function selfishly. Their workings will be grace for the good of all. The fragmentary "I" is lost forever. His ego can never revive. Therefore he is said to be liberated here and now. He does not live because his body lives, nor does he die because his body dies. He is eternal. There is nothing other than he. You are He.

10. Who is God? He is grace. What is Grace? Awareness without the fragmentary ego. How can one know that there is such a state? Only if one realizes it. The Vedas laud such a one as having realized God and become one with Him. Therefore

the greatest good that one can derive from the world and the greatest good which one can render unto it, is to realize this state. In fact, there are no states besides this. They appear in the state of ignorance. For him who knows, there is one state only. You are that.

Commentary

1. Who are you? Are you this body? If so, why are you not aware of a serpent crawling on it when you are in deep sleep? So then can you be this body? No, certainly not. You must be other than this body.

In the same way: Are you aware of the entire range of creation? Are you experiencing yourself at this moment as actually *being* the entire range of creation–and also even beyond it? Of course not. So just because you are one with Brahman does not mean you are Brahman in the absolute sense. An object that is gold is just an infinitesimal part of the gold of the world. Certainly the object could say, "I am gold," but it could never say, "I am gold" in the sense of being all the gold of the world. That would be crazy, and a lot of people *are* crazy–at least speaking and acting so. These are the people that Swami Krishnananda, Secretary of the Divine Life Society, used to call "trained Vedantic thugs." We must avoid being the same or even giving the impression that we are.

I hope that my insistence on this is not annoying, but this absurd, egoic delusion is being sought after by many, and is being claimed by many, including some who claim to be following Sri Ramana Maharshi who recommended this book. They are like

Alan Ginsberg. When he told Swami Sivananda that he was looking for a guru, Sivanandaji said, "You are the guru." So he came back and told people that Sivananda had declared him the guru of America! They credit their delusions to Sri Ramana, whom they often claim is their guru.

2. Sometimes in sleep you dream. There you identify yourself with someone. Can you be that one? You cannot be. Otherwise, what becomes of that individual on your waking? You are not he. Furthermore, you are ashamed of having identified yourself with him. Clearly, you are not that particular person. You are the one that stands apart from him.

It has almost always been my experience that in dream I am my waking self, though usually in circumstances that were different from the waking state. And occasionally I have dreamed I was someone else. In any dream I have usually known it was a dream. And I think this is not uncommon, for in a way reflects the three possible states of understanding: 1) being completely immersed in a false experience, 2) being only partly immersed in that experience, 3) fully aware that the experience is false and not identifying with it in any manner.

The great need is to be always awake. And that is only possible for an adept yogi. Just thinking or reading about it accomplishes nothing. It is a state of consciousness that anyone can claim, but few really have.

3. Recall the state of dreamless slumber. What is your state then? Can that be your true nature? Surely you will not subscribe to this belief. Why? Because you are not so foolish as to identify yourself with the massive darkness which obstructs you from knowing the state you are in. Discerned by the intellect from the things around, how can you admit yourself to be the same as ignorance or blank? Or, how can it truly be your real nature? It cannot be. You are the knower who knows that this state remains one of dense darkness veiling your true nature. How can you be that which you have experienced and condemned? Therefore you are not the dark ignorance of deep sleep. You stand apart from this too.

Frankly, I always experienced this as a witness. I could have done nothing other, as I never forgot who I was.

I do not believe that anyone thinks of themselves as the experience they are witnessing, though they believe in the reality of the experience. Rather, at that point they do not think of who they are. But that is not forgetting, it is just not considering it relevant at the moment. And deep sleep is not ignorance, only lack of perception and memory. Since this is essential for health of the body, to disdain or somehow condemn it is foolish.

I have never thought that either the dreamless or dreaming states were natural to me, considering that two-thirds of my continuous experience and memory were of the waking state. That I identified with the body and the circumstances in which I found myself, such as my name and relation to the things in my environment, was inevitable, and from that I needed to awaken. Then dream and dreamless would be seen as mirages in my mind—as was my waking state. I used to ponder this when I was three and four years old.

No author or book is infallible, and frankly I consider the wording of this and the previous proposition as bordering on the fatuous, though the eventual conclusions are sound.

4. When it is said that even this gross body is not you, can you be any other thing which is yet farther away from you? In the same way that you are not this gross body, you are not anything farther from the body, nor the dream person, nor the ignorance of deep sleep. You are distinct from these three states and this world.

The author of *Ellam Ondre* was no doubt Tamil, and what was then called Madras State was the home of the headquarters of the Theosophical Society which considered Sanatana Dharma as the fundamental truth about relative existence and the human being. The Theosophists did not just briefly tip their hats to Sanatana Dharma, they bowed their heads before it and extolled it. Consequently the author did not want to show any disrespect to them. But here he had to mention their unacceptable view about the Self, the essential being of the individual person. They postulated that the real Self was literally high above the body and was connected to it by subtle astral and causal energy bonds, that the Self was never really incarnated at any time. Other Western metaphysicians postulated that the Self was even in another world of its own and only experienced this world as a dream projected from itself. They not only said we were not the body, mind and senses, they said we were not even here at all, but were far, far beyond or above any relative existence at all.

The truth is, we are distinct from the three states of relative consciousness and this world, but we are not separate and outside them. Rather, we are in them as their reality, their very core. Separate from us they cannot exist. Since we ourselves are one with the Being of Brahman, it could not be otherwise.

5. These three states can be reduced to two conditions only—namely, the one of the subject and object, and the other is the unawareness of the subject itself. The former includes the waking and dream states, whereas the latter represents deep slumber. All your experiences are comprised in these two conditions only. Both of them are foreign to you. Your true nature remains distinct from them.

I have no idea why the author did not simply use the terms waking, dreaming and deep sleep as the fundamental three states of the embodied consciousness. But he has pointed out the two essential conditions of those experiencing them: 1) awareness only of the object perceived, and 2) awareness of both the object and the perceiver of the object. And this is a very insightful distillation of the result of these two conditions: remembrance and forgetfulness.

It is only natural that we remember and forget the experiencing of objects throughout our life, but it is the supreme defect to ever for a moment forget our own Self, the experiencer. We are the Self, never the object, and yet we identify with the object and forget and even deny the existence of the Self.

Because of their evanescent character all objects are ultimately unexistent/unreal, and the Self is the sole reality, the only truth. That is why when someone asked Shankara, "What is truth (satya)?" he replied, "There is no truth (satya)—only the Sat." Knowing this, as a perfected yogi (see *The Christ of India*), Jesus did not answer Pilate when Pilate asked him "What is truth?" (John 18:37-38).

The third, true/real experience is that of the Self alone, awareness that the experiencing, the experience and the experiencer are at all times ONE. For there is nothing but the One. And that implies that even the conditions of delusion and illusion are projections of our own consciousness and therefore are also part of the One. The idea to rid ourselves of these errors is a mistake. What we need to experience is their essential reality as only consciousness–nothing else. And consciousness by its nature is absolutely unitary: One in essence. This is why the sages have said that all of relative existence is the play of Consciousness. It may be illusion, but it is a real illusion, a projection of Consciousness. Beyond understanding this is becoming It. That we must aspire to. "Therefore be a yogi" (Bhagavad Gita 6:46).

6. If you ask what that is, it is called turiya, which means the fourth state. Why is this name used? This name is proper because it seems to say the three states of your experience–waking, dream and deep sleep–are foreign to you and your true state is the fourth, which is different from these three. Should the three states, waking, dream and deep sleep, be taken to form one long dream, the fourth state represents the waking from this dream. Thus it is more withdrawn than deep sleep, also more wakeful than the waking state.

This encapsulation is a miracle of intelligence and insight. It is so simple and yet so vast that I need to divide it into separate portions that must eventually be reunited into a single realization.

If you ask what that is, it is called turiya, which means the fourth state. Why is this name used? This name is proper because it seems to say the three states of your experience—waking, dream and deep sleep—are foreign to you and your true state is the fourth, which is different from these three. Should the three states, waking, dream and deep sleep, be taken to form one long dream, the fourth state represents the waking from this dream.

This I think is clear to us all at this point in our consideration.

Thus it is more withdrawn than deep sleep, also more wakeful than the waking state.

Now this is extremely important, because we tend to take our own characteristics and assume that perfection is the expansion of them to the maximum scope or intensity. But this is not wisdom. Here we are being told that turiya is far more conscious than our present condition of being awake and conscious, and it is also far deeper, profound and beyond external experience than our present deep sleep state. For in its essence turiya is not an expansion of these conditions, but a transcending of all our three usual states of consciousness.

Therefore your true state is that fourth one which is distinguished from the waking, dream and deep sleep states.

It does not embrace or include these three states, but is beyond them while at the same time being the very basis of their existence/experience.

You are that only.

How easy to say. And how impossible to comprehend, much less attain, for anyone who is not transmuting his consciousness through intense yoga sadhana. In some books attributed to

Shankara a disciple asks a question and the teacher explains the answer very thoroughly. Then the disciple immediately launches into a kind of self-eulogy that rapturously goes on and on about how he now has entered into cosmic consciousness and knows himself as the One. Supposedly the teaching itself has liberated him and made him a sage and a siddha. Not likely. That is like claiming indigestion from reading a recipe in a cookbook. Hearing, thinking and believing (and imagining!) is not experiential knowledge.

7. What is this fourth state? It is knowledge which does not particularize anything. It is not unaware of itself. That is to say, the fourth state is Pure Knowledge which is not conscious of any object, but not unconscious itself. Only he who has realized it even for a trice, has realized the Truth. You are that only.

This is absolutely true, but those who have not had at least a mild experience or glimpse of this state cannot even imagine what is meant by this statement. In fact those who try to understand it will most certainly be sure to misunderstand it.

For example, the statement that turiya "does not particularize anything" is thought to mean that the realized person sees everything as the same and makes no distinction between anything. If that was so, he would readily drink poison as freely as he drinks water. He would accept anything no matter how detrimental or destructive. He would be a fool. The author means that he sees that all things are manifestations of the One. But the very fact that the One has made infinite differentiations means that we are to respond to them in different ways even though we realize the underlying unity.

The principle that "Pure Knowledge is not conscious of any object" is thought by the ignorant to mean that the realized individual is less than a newborn infant—for the infant sees various objects through he does not name or classify them. They think that the siddha does not ever experience things, that even though he moves around, speaks to people, answers questions and does various actions he is not aware of it, being somewhere "off in space" alone and aware only of emptiness. I have read incredibly absurd descriptions of what "devotees" thought was the habitual condition or experience of both Ramana Maharshi and Anandamayi Ma. Mere intellectual speculation in relation to these sublime realities can only lead to fantasy. The simple advice Grow Up is thoroughly applicable to such childish egos.

The state of perfect realization is what Vyasa describes in the Bhagavad Gita as: "innermost secret: knowledge of God which is nearer than knowing, open vision direct and instant" (9:1). It cannot be spoken about in any manner except to say that it cannot be spoken about. That is why the Kena Upanishad says: "To whomsoever It [Brahman] is not known, to him It is known: to whomsoever It is known, he does not know. It is not understood by those who understand It; it is understood by those who do not understand it" (2.3). The interpretive translation by Prabhavananda make this clear: "He truly knows Brahman who knows him as beyond knowledge; he who thinks that he knows, knows not. The ignorant think that Brahman is known, but the wise know him to be beyond knowledge."

In other words: "He who knows tells it not; he who tells knows it not." If we do not make these words a realization rather than a philosophical maxim or speculation we have missed the idea altogether. For often the words of the wise about the highest matters sound absurd, but that is only because our experiences and thinking has heretofore been utterly absurd. So in the context of our absurdity truth appears absurd. This is the terrible illusion and blindness of the unawake individual.

8. What is there more for him who has gained the fourth state? Practically, it is not possible for anyone to remain forever in that state, that is, the state of no particular knowledge. He who has realized the fourth state later wakes up in this world, but for him this world is not as before. He sees that what he realized as the fourth state, shines forth as all this. He will not imagine this world as distinct from that Pure Knowledge. Thus what he saw within, he now sees without in a different form. In the place of the differentiation of old, he is now established in the state of non-differentiation everywhere. Now, he is all. There is nothing distinct from himself. His eyes closed or open, howsoever the things may change, his state remains unchanged. This is the state of Brahman. This is the natural eternal state. You are that ever-true state.

This is also a miracle of clarity and illumined reason. Let us look at it in pieces.

What is there more for him who has gained the fourth state?
Nothing.

Practically, it is not possible for anyone to remain forever in that state, that is, the state of no particular knowledge.

It is not possible in this world, though in higher worlds it is the only possible permanent state. That is why in meditation the yogi clearly perceives all spiritual realities and their implications, but when he leaves meditation he comes down to a lower plane of experience and knows he cannot act in accordance with his insights because what he perceived in meditation, even though in the body, is inapplicable to the mundane life of the mundane world. But he does not forget what he has perceived.

He who has realized the fourth state later wakes up in this world, but for him this world is not as before. I remember a man speaking of his spiritual awakening and saying, "To me the whole world was different. But then I realized the truth: the world was the same, but *I* was different." Rather simple, really.

He sees that what he realized as the fourth state, shines forth as all this.

The world has not become turiya, it always was turiya. But that had to be directly seen and comprehended (realized). And from now on the awakened sees that all is turiya, including himself. It always was.

He will not imagine this world as distinct from that Pure Knowledge. Thus what he saw within, he now sees without in a different form. In the place of the differentiation of old, he is now established in the state of non-differentiation everywhere. Now, he is all. There is nothing distinct from himself. His eyes closed or open, howsoever the things may change, his state remains unchanged. This is the state of Brahman. This is the natural eternal state. You are that ever-true state.

What is more wonderful, more thrilling than this glorious truth? Sri Sanatana Dharma: Ki Jai!!!

9. *There is nothing beyond this state. The words, "inward" and "outward" have no meaning for him. All is one. His body, speech and mind cannot function selfishly. Their workings will be grace for the good of all. The fragmentary "I" is lost forever. His ego can never revive. Therefore he is said to be liberated here and now. He does not live because his body lives, nor does he die because his body dies. He is eternal. There is nothing other than he. You are He.*

10. *Who is God? He is grace. What is Grace? Awareness without the fragmentary ego. How can one know that there is such a state? Only if one realizes it. The Vedas laud such a one as having realized God and become one with Him. Therefore the greatest good that one can derive from the world and the greatest good which one can render unto it, is to realize this state. In fact, there are no states besides this. They appear in the state of ignorance. For him who knows, there is one state only. You are that.*

I dare not touch these two sublime and awesome statements with words of mine. They are perfect and complete.

CHAPTER THREE–GOD

1. Who is God? God is He who has transcended all that is seen by us. If transcending this world, is there no relation between Him and this world? Not a particle here is unrelated to Him. Then what is meant by transcending the world? The world comprises us and the objects seen by us. In other words, the animate and inanimate together form the world. What shall we say of Him who created the beings and things? Of these two, we say the conscious beings to be superior. All that we can apprehend is that He belongs to the highest order of beings known to us. Our intellect cannot proceed further. Thus, our Creator is superior to us; He cannot be apprehended by our intellect; therefore His Name, Transcended Being, "Kadawul," means that He surpasses our intellect. Hence His Name is "Kadawul"–Transcended Being.

2. Can God then not be made known to us? Not quite so. In a way, He is known to us. This much of His Grace is enough for us. We have no need for all His Greatness. He has made known so much of His Greatness as will suffice to eradicate our misery. There is no reason for Him to reveal a jot more of His Power than is necessary to remedy our defects in the present state. Thus He is known according to our needs. Nay, He is in our grasp. However limitless, He is within reach of our knowledge to some extent.

3. What is it which brings Him within reach of our knowledge? That He is known as Being-Consciousness-Bliss.

Being denotes that which is imperishable, that which exists forever. Should He become nonexistent at any time, who is His Destroyer? Who created Him? Since the perishable nature of all leads to the inference that they are lorded over by One who is imperishable, this immortal Overlord is God. His imperishable nature is Being (Sat).

Now, what is Consciousness (Chit)? By Consciousness we mean knowledge. This is absolute Knowledge, and not like our erring intellectual knowledge. Irregularity or mistake cannot stain its actions. It is Knowledge, pure and simple. Frequently He teaches us saying, "Your knowledge is irregular and erring." How orderly are even the insentient objects of His creation! It is known to many how an atheist was taught a good lesson when he derided the scheme of things saying, "Why did He make the seed so small for the banyan tree which is so big?" That an insentient thing is found in good order and later becomes useful, implies a conscious agency at work. Can a simple, insentient thing do something which is possible for unfailing knowledge only? Or, can't it be done by our inadequate knowledge? No, it can never be. Therefore God is said to be Consciousness (Chit) also.

Now, what is Bliss? It is the state of being free from desire for anything. It is Peace which is ever full. Were He to desire anything, how could He be better than ourselves? How could we gain Bliss from Him? He Himself would require another being to fulfill His desires. But who would think Him to be so? The state of self-contentment is that of Bliss also. Therefore He is called Bliss (Ananda).

The three–Being, Consciousness and Bliss–are inseparable; otherwise, they would become naught individually. Hence, He is known as Being-Consciousness-Bliss (Sat-Chit-Ananda). Thus God remains not only transcendent but also falls within the reach of our knowledge as Being-Consciousness-Bliss.

4. He who has gained the fourth state and sees all as one, only he knows God truly as Being-Consciousness-Bliss. Words cannot express nor the ears hear how such a one is united with God; it is a matter of realization. But there are ways and means for such realization. They can be spoken of, learned and acted upon.

5. He who can be realized thus, is God. He has no name; we give Him a name. He has no form; we give Him a form. Where is the harm in doing so? What name is not His, or what form is not His? Where is the sound or form in which He is not? Therefore, in the absence of true knowledge of Him you can name Him as you please or imagine Him as of any form so to remember Him. Your hope for His Grace without any effort on your part is utterly fruitless. Should it be possible to have His Grace without any effort on your side, all would be alike; there would be no reason for any difference. He has shown us the ways and means. Make effort, reach the goal, be happy. Your idleness and selfishness make you expect His Grace without your effort. The rule for all is for you too. Do not relax your efforts. God can be realized by your effort only.

6. There is an effort which excels all others. This may, however, appear to be less effective than devotion to God with name and form. Nevertheless, this is the more efficient. It is simply the love which you extend to all beings, whether good or bad. In

the absence of such love to all, your devotion to God amounts to a mere parody. Of what use are you to God? That you seek fulfillment of your desires from God without doing your duty towards the needy in the world must be attributed to your self-ishness. In God's presence, there is no use for such. The workings that take place in His presence are all unselfish. Therefore, think that all the Centers are His and He is in all the Centers and thus be devoted to Him. God is truly bound by such high devotion.

7. As you go on ascribing names and forms to God and showing love to all because you have understood all names and forms to be His, your mind will gradually mature. Just as the taste improves with the ripening of a fruit, so also you will recognize the waxing of good and the waning of evil in you. As your mind matures, there will come a time when you should meet your Master. This is not to say that you go in search of him or he comes in search of you. At the right time the meeting will happen. All are moving in their own ways. Your fitness brings you together, makes you trust him, makes him teach you the right way, also makes you follow his instructions. That is the straight way to reach God, which is to gain the fourth state. You will follow the way and reach your goal which is Being-Con-sciousness-Bliss, which is God.

8. The way shown by the Master is final, straight and making for unity. It is well-tried, natural, and free from pain. When you are following the way shown by the master, doubts will not arise; there will be no fear. Are not fear and doubt the characteristics of the ways of darkness? How can they meet you in the way of Truth shown by the Master? In this manner, the way will itself

speak to you and say that it is the right one. In that way, there will be nothing more for you to do but to meet your Master and learn from him. That way will be familiar to you, as the Master and God have made it so. Before you, he had treaded the way. He has shown you the way and you are following him. To how many will you show the same way? And how many more will follow the same way later? Obviously fear and doubt have no place in the way of truth. When once you have taken a step forward you will step back. The master's help is only for the first step forward. You need not do anything for your master in order to have the way shown to you. Know him to be the messenger of God sent down to disclose the way to the fit who have become ripe by their own efforts in either or both the directions mentioned earlier. It is God who sends this godly messenger just when you are ripe.

9. Practice with faith in the period of ignorance is called Bhakti (path of Devotion); the same, with knowledge, is called Jnana (the path of Wisdom). Of the two divisions of Bhakti, the one is devotion to God with name and form, and the other is karma which is love for all. Of the two divisions of Jnana, the practice of the true way shown by the Master is called yoga and the resulting state is called Jnana (knowledge). It is natural for all to believe in something which is not seen and then to find it. Those who do not believe can never find. Therefore, the believers will gain something sometime or other and the unbelievers never gain anything. You can believe even for the simple reason that faith in God is not harmful. Thereby you can share the good effects. This world is meant only for creating faith in you. This is the purpose of creation. Have faith and you can reach God.

10. Though you may not believe all that is said of God, believe at least "There is God." This seed is very potent in its growth. It is so mighty as to negate all else and fill all by itself. It is so almighty that you will not see anything besides God, not even yourself. Truly, God is all.

Commentary

Before considering this section I need to state that it is not known what Sanskrit word is being translated as "God." Since God is referred to as "our Creator" and "His Grace" is mentioned, whatever the word this obviously refers to Ishwara, the "personal" consciousness that pervades the cosmos and guides its evolution along with the evolution of all sentient beings within it. The title "Bhagavan" is applicable also. These words are defined in *A Brief Sanskrit Glossary* as follows:

Ishwara: "God" or "Lord" in the sense of the Supreme Power, Ruler, Master or Controller of the cosmos. "Ishwara" implies the powers of omnipotence, omnipresence and omniscience.

Bhagavan: The Lord; the One endowed with the attributes: infinite dominion, infinite might, infinite glory, infinite splendor, infinite wisdom and infinite renunciation; the Personal God.

1. Who is God? God is He who has transcended all that is seen by us. If transcending this world, is there no relation between Him and this world? Not a particle here is unrelated to Him. Then what is meant by transcending the world? The world comprises us and the objects seen by us. In other words, the animate and inanimate together form the world. What shall we say of Him who created the beings and things? Of these two, we say the conscious beings to be superior. All that we can apprehend is that He belongs to the highest order of beings known to us. Our intellect cannot proceed further. Thus, our Creator is superior to us; He cannot be apprehended by our intellect; therefore His Name, Transcendent Being, "Kadawul," means that He surpasses our intellect. Hence His Name is "Kad-awul"–Transcendent Being.

God is He who has transcended all that is seen by us. This implies that God–Ishwara/Bhagavan once was a relative being himself within this creation and having transcended the realm of relative existence is now pervading it as its inner controller and fosterer. Whether this is His "yoga" by which He is continuing to evolve to Infinity, or whether He is already in the infinite state right now is not known, but some people in India hold one view or the other. Actually, it is irrelevant to us, for we are following the usual path that leads up to Infinity without requiring that we be Ishwaras/Bhagavans ourself as part of the enlightenment process. Fortunately we do not all have to spend creation cycles being Ishwaras/Bhagavans.

The rest of this verse is quite clear and needs no comment by me except to point out that every particle of every atom in this creation in which we find ourselves (and there are many creations–this is but one of them) is in intimate relation with God, and that the idea we must seek God or establish some personal relation with Him is ridiculous. We already have that relation. Rather, we must cooperate with Him and eventually awaken in his Light so we can pass onward to Infinity as did He Himself some time in the past.

By the way, Kadawul is a Tamil word, not Sanskrit, so it will not be found in any Sanskrit dictionary.

2. Can God then not be made known to us? Not quite so. In a way, He is known to us. This much of His Grace is enough for us. We have no need for all His Greatness. He has made known so much of His Greatness as will suffice to eradicate our misery. There is no reason for Him to reveal a jot more of His Power than is necessary to remedy our defects in the present state. Thus He is known according to our needs. Nay, He is in our grasp. However limitless, He is within reach of our knowledge to some extent.

Can God then not be made known to us? Not quite so. In a way, He is known to us. Since God is all-pervading consciousness, there is nothing that is unknown to Him. Even more important is that fact that His mind is in total contact with our mind, and it works both ways. In the ultimate heights or depths of our consciousness we are in contact with his consciousness. But presently we are only subliminally or potentially aware of his consciousness, and so we must awaken to/into it insofar as we are capable. That is, we will only have a finite scope to that awareness, we will not suddenly become infinite ourselves. A reflection in a mirror is not the thing that is reflected. When we stand on the shore of the ocean, facing the ocean, we can say, "I see the ocean." But we are really only seeing a tiny part, a speck, of the vast ocean. So we both do and do not see it, since we do not see the whole thing.

This much of His Grace is enough for us. We have no need for all His Greatness.

That is, we do not–and cannot–know the whole of God's consciousness as He does the whole of our consciousness. But what we can know of Him in the form of a deep intuition is sufficient to help us by stimulating us to consciously move onward in the evolution/expansion of the scope of our present state of consciousness, to reflect His eternal being. We do not need to know all about God (we cannot) and all His glories and powers–only that which relates to our own evolution and eventually perfect Realization.

Sri Ramakrishna said: "The one thing you need is to realize God. Why do you bother so much about the world, creation, 'science,' and all that? Your business is to eat mangoes [realize God]. What need have you to know how many hundreds of trees there are in the orchard, how many thousands of branches, and how many millions of leaves? You have come to the garden to eat mangoes. Go and eat them. Man is born in this world to realize God; it is not good to forget that and divert the mind to other things. You have come to eat mangoes. Eat the mangoes and be happy."

He has made known so much of His Greatness as will suffice to eradicate our misery. There is no reason for Him to reveal a jot more of His Power than is necessary to remedy our defects in the present state. Thus He is known according to our needs.

This says it all.

Nay, He is in our grasp. However limitless, He is within reach of our knowledge to some extent.

This is all we need to know—and act upon. We are inseparable from God in our inmost being. Therefore to know God we need only know our Self which is one with God. Yoga is the one essential to do so.

3. What is it which brings Him within reach of our knowledge? That He is known as Being-Consciousness-Bliss [Satchidananda].

Being denotes that which is imperishable, that which exists forever. Should He become nonexistent at any time, who is His Destroyer? Who created Him? Since the perishable nature of all leads to the inference that they are lorded over by One who is imperishable, this immortal Overlord is God. His imperishable nature is Being (Sat).

Now, what is Consciousness (Chit)? By Consciousness we mean knowledge. This is absolute Knowledge, and not like our erring intellectual knowledge. Irregularity or mistake cannot stain its actions. It is Knowledge, pure and simple. Frequently He teaches us saying, "Your knowledge is irregular and erring." How orderly are even the insentient objects of His creation! It is known to many how an atheist was taught a good lesson when he derided the scheme of things saying, "Why did He make the seed so small for the banyan tree which is so big?" [This must refer to a story commonly known in Tamilnad, so he does not relay it.] That an insentient thing is found in good order and later becomes useful, implies a conscious agency at work. Can a simple, insentient thing do something which is possible for unfailing knowledge only? Or, can't it be done by our inadequate knowledge? No, it can never be. Therefore God is said to be Consciousness (Chit) also.

Now, what is Bliss? It is the state of being free from desire for anything. It is Peace which is ever full. Were He to desire anything, how could He be better than ourselves? How could we gain Bliss from Him? He Himself would require another being to fulfill His desires. But who would think Him to be so? The state of self-contentment is that of Bliss also. Therefore He is called Bliss (Ananda).

The three—Being, Consciousness and Bliss—are inseparable; otherwise, they would become naught individually. Hence, He is known as Being-Consciousness-Bliss (Sat-Chit-Ananda). Thus God remains not only transcendent but also falls within the reach of our knowledge as Being-Consciousness-Bliss.

It is a wise child that knows its father, and I am wise enough to know I cannot improve upon this by any commentary.

4. He who has gained the fourth state [of turiya] and sees all as one, only he knows God truly as Being-Consciousness-Bliss. Words cannot express nor the ears hear how such a one is united with God; it is a matter of realization.

As the venerable saying goes: Talk Does Not Cook The Rice. Nor does merely reading books such as *Ellam Ondre* and "believing" them without acting upon their precepts. Talking about the ideas of such books and going on and on about them in order to appear wise and a "serious seeker" is pure folly and leads nowhere but into the ego.

But there are ways and means for such realization. They can be spoken of, learned and acted upon.

The ways and means for realization are the learning and the practice of true yoga: Soham Sadhana. Nothing else. That is why Sri Ramana Maharshi wrote in his commentary on *Devikallotara Jnanachara Vichara Padalam*: "Soham Sadhana is the last pilgrimage.... Meditate thus for a long time on the Self."

5. He who can be realized thus, is God. He has no name; we give Him a name. He has no form; we give Him a form. Where is the harm in doing so? What name is not His, or what form is not His? Where is the sound or form in which He is not? Therefore, in the absence of true knowledge of Him you can name Him as you please or imagine Him as of any form so to remember Him. Your hope for His Grace without any effort on your part is utterly fruitless. Should it be possible to have His Grace without any effort on your side, all would be alike; there would be no reason for any difference. He has shown us the ways and means. Make effort, reach the goal, be happy. Your idleness and selfishness make you expect His Grace without your effort. The rule for all is for you too. Do not relax your efforts. God can be realized by your effort only.

He who can be realized thus, is God.

Here we have the essence of all wisdom: God can be realized through Yoga Sadhana—Soham Sadhana specifically. I myself am doing it and I recommend that you do it also. Read *Soham Yoga: The Yoga of the Self* and *Light of Soham*.

He has no name; we give Him a name. He has no form; we give Him a form. Where is the harm in doing so? What name is not His, or what form is not His? Where is the sound or form in which He is not? Therefore, in the absence of true knowledge of Him you can name Him as you please or imagine Him as of any form so to remember Him.

This is quite revolutionary if you are used to the narrow, elitist Advaita platitudes (More Non-dual Than Thou) and the disdain of "bothering" with name and form in your relation (or attempted relation) with God since essentially God has no name or form. But as the author rightly points out, since in the realm of projected relativity all names and forms are God's, there is no violation of truth or spiritual law by attributing name and form to God as long as we do not confuse them with the eternal reality of God's nature, and we intend to in time go beyond these symbols into encounter with the Reality to which they point us. It is very much like the common observance that if we get a thorn in our foot we can take it out by means of another thorn and then need neither of them any longer. In the same way, since we are immersed in and even addicted to name and form we can attribute them to God and by continued concentration on them as symbols of Him reach beyond them to Whom they represent.

Your hope for His Grace without any effort on your part is utterly fruitless.

Once someone asked Yogananda for his blessing. Yogananda replied: "You already have God's blessing and you have my blessing. What you lack is your blessing." The truth is that we have nothing but grace from God at all times, and part of that grace is the ability to save ourselves through yoga sadhana. Our free will is a gift of God that cannot fail when diligently applied in the right manner and in the right direction.

Several times in my writings I have mentioned a cartoon I saw long ago in which a drunk was lying in the gutter while a Salvation Army lady was bending over him. The caption was: "Do I have to go somewhere, or can you save me here?" This is the way of the incorrigible, the "invincibly ignorant." They do not want to do any thing, but have it all done for them. It will not happen.

When I was a novice in an Athonite monastery the abbot told me that at his first meeting with a great spiritual director (elder) he had asked him, "Please pray for me." "No," said the holy man. "I cannot eat for you or breathe or sleep for you, so I cannot pray for you. You must pray for yourself." As Saint Paul wrote, "Awake thou that sleepest, and arise" (Ephesians 5:14). And the Prodigal Son, realizing his degraded condition resolved: "I will arise and go" (Luke 15:18). As the hymn says: "O soul, be up and doing, you have no time to lose. There is life and death before you: O which one will you choose?"

It is all up to us to awake and arise. The ability to awake and arise is Grace, but we must match that grace and save (liberate) ourselves. Passive trust in God gets us nowhere.

Should it be possible to have His Grace without any effort on your side, all would be alike; there would be no reason for any difference.

The grace of God if active in all would long ago have brought all to liberation. Sri Gajanana Maharaj (see *Light of Soham*) pointed out that since saints are one with God and are pure vessels of his love, if it were possible for a saint to save anyone, they would long ago have done so, and all would be liberated alike.

He has shown us the ways and means.
Dharma and Yoga are the ways and means: Right Living and Right Meditation, to use Buddha's terms.

Make effort, reach the goal, be happy.
This is the only true order of the path to liberation. First we make effort, then we begin to attain to higher consciousness and then we enjoy the bliss of the Self. But first and foremost is effort in the form of following the principles of dharma and continually being engaged in the process of yoga sadhana.

Your idleness and selfishness make you expect His Grace without your effort.
Until we eliminate this laziness and self-indulgence the grace of God cannot really reach us and work in us to attainment of the Divine Goal.

The rule for all is for you too.
We all want God to "make an exception" in our case and and give us liberation just because we think we want it. But we do not—our inactivity proves that. How amazing it is that we acknowledge the need for effort to attain our small, short term

goals in what we call "my life," but in the matter of attaining the Absolute Consciousness we claim that we should not be required to do anything but just "receive" God's grace. It will not work.

Do not relax your efforts. God can be realized by your effort only.
Again: the only "saving grace" is our own grace on ourselves by our working to achieve Infinity through yoga sadhana. We must not hesitate or stop, we must move ahead intent on the Goal.

6. There is an effort which excels all others. This may, however, appear to be less effective than devotion to God with name and form. Nevertheless, this is the more efficient. It is simply the love which you extend to all beings, whether good or bad. In the absence of such love to all, your devotion to God amounts to a mere parody. Of what use are you to God? That you seek fulfillment of your desires from God without doing your duty towards the needy in the world must be attributed to your selfishness. In God's presence, there is no use for such. The workings that take place in His presence are all unselfish. Therefore, think that all the Centers are His and He is in all the Centers and thus be devoted to Him. God is truly bound by such high devotion.

There is an effort which excels all others. This may, however, appear to be less effective than devotion to God with name and form. Nevertheless, this is the more efficient.
This is very important, because the author is preparing us for facts of life in this world that extend into the realm of the

spirit and render us capable of higher life in relation to God. And I must say that I have never found this perspective in any other book on spiritual matters, whatever the religious tradition might be.

It is simply the love which you extend to all beings, whether good or bad.

To love all, whether they are positive or negative, is a tremendous goal for anyone to set for themselves. In fact, it is impossible for anyone who is not methodically and continuously awakening and expanding all their faculties, including those of the heart. And whatever may be claimed for others, I can tell you absolutely that no one but an adept yogi could possibly attain this universal love.

Love is faked up all the time under the veneer of emotion and external actions made to appear as love—which is not difficult considering that very few in this world even know what true love is. So I can assure you that only those already a goodly distance along the upward path can possibly develop such an all-embracing love. I have only seen one person in my life that was capable of such vast love, and that was Swami Sivananda of Rishikesh, the supreme master of yoga.

However, every sadhaka must aspire to this ability and work toward it through his sadhana and his contact with others daily.

In the absence of such love to all, your devotion to God amounts to a mere parody.

This is because God is present in every atom of creation and especially in the heart of every sentient being. In the Bhagavad Gita we are told, "The Lord lives in the heart of every creature" (Bhagavad Gita 18:61). And God himself says: "I am the Atman [Self] that dwells in the heart of every mortal creature" (Bhagavad Gita 10:20). "I am in all hearts" (Bhagavad Gita 15:15). Therefore, if we do not love all we do not love God. And we should admit it if we do not so love, and keep on with our sadhana until that capacity arises in our expanding consciousness. This is no time or place for Let's Pretend. For God tells us: "Who[ever] burns with the bliss and suffers the sorrow of every creature within his own heart, making his own each bliss and each sorrow: him I hold highest of all the yogis" (Bhagavad Gita 6:32).

Of what use are you to God?

God is drawing all beings toward himself from within, and those that love all beings with God's love are his instruments by which he draws them to himself from without. Both are needed, and we alone can assist God in the second mode of drawing. Then we will be gods and parts of the love of God.

That you seek fulfillment of your desires from God without doing your duty towards the needy in the world must be attributed to your selfishness. In God's presence, there is no use for such. The workings that take place in His presence are all unselfish. Therefore, think that all the Centers are His and He is in all the Centers and thus be devoted to Him. God is truly bound by such high devotion.

By "Centers" the author means all living beings, for God dwells in their inmost being, making them centers of his indwelling. Since we are part of those centers, God is already in our heart awaiting our awakening to his presence from which his love can go forth to every atom in this universe, especially to the heart of every human being. This is true bhakti, true devotion to God, otherwise as already said, our devotion to God "amounts to a mere parody."

This is a high ideal. How can we fulfill it? Saint Thomas Aquinas was asked the same question, and his answer was simple and direct: "Will it." Our will is the highest personal power we possess, and we should use it to become and manifest the Universal Love that is God.

How do we do it? "Therefore be a yogi" (Bhagavad Gita 6:46).

7. As you go on ascribing names and forms to God and showing love to all because you have understood all names and forms to be His, your mind will gradually mature.

This is the real evolution we seek. Many think that it is merely stacking up intellectual philosophical and religious ideas and repeating them while doing "good" in a rote, but not heart-felt, manner. Such is expansion of the ego, not evolution of our consciousness.

Only by our love for all beings in God can we really grow into our full potential as gods within God. Why, then, do we become yogis and meditate? Because true meditation, true yoga sadhana, purifies the heart and enables it to expand and evolve. And we must realize that fixing the awareness on the

Divine Self within us during meditation is the highest form of loving God who is the Self of our Self. And continuing outside meditation to center our mind on God through the sacred japa of Soham in time with the breath is also the highest form of loving God. Again: see *Soham Yoga: The Yoga of the Self* and *Light of Soham*.

Only those who love can expand and grow.

Just as the taste improves with the ripening of a fruit, so also you will recognize the waxing of good and the waning of evil in you.

There is no place here for blinding ourselves to the fact that we are a mixture of positive and negative, and as yogis must become keenly aware of these two elements and continually apply the practice of sadhana for the increase of the positive and the decrease (eventually total annihilation) of the negative. In other words, we are to be watching our inner and outer being at all times and honestly evaluating what we find there while applying ourselves to continuous inner construction by Soham Yoga meditation and japa.

I have mentioned Soham Yoga so much that I should pause now to give you the teaching of Sri Ramana Maharshi on the matter.

Sri Ramana Maharshi and Soham Sadhana

Someone asked Bhagavan Sri Ramana Maharshi: "What is the purport of the teaching that one should meditate, through the 'I am That' thought, on the truth that one is not different from the self-luminous Reality that shines like a flame?"

Bhagavan replied: "The purport of teaching that one should meditate with the 'I am That' thought is this: *sah-aham*: So'ham; *sah* the supreme Self, *aham* the Self that is manifest as 'I.' If one meditates for a long time, without disturbance, on the Self ceaselessly, with the 'So'ham–I am That' thought which is the technique of reflection on the Self, the darkness of ignorance which is in the heart and all the impediments which are but the effects of ignorance will be removed, and the plenary wisdom will be gained…. The body is the temple; the jiva is God (Shiva). If one worships him with the 'So'ham–I am That' thought, one will gain release" (*Collected Works* [Section] 29).

Once Bhagavan Sri Ramana Maharshi was shown the Sanskrit text of *Devikallotara Jnanachara Vichara Padalam* (A Study of the Exposition of Supreme Wisdom and Conduct to Goddess Ishwari by Lord Shiva) written on palm leaves. He said that this writing was very, very important, and himself translated it into Tamil with his commentary. Sri T. K. Jayaram then translated it into English, including the following:

"[Shiva said to Parvati:] The means by which this mind, which is restless and moves about quicker than the wind, can be brought under control, is indeed the means to obtain liberation; is indeed what is good for those who seek permanent Reality; it itself is pure Consciousness and the state of firmness; moreover, it alone is the righteous duty to be followed by discerning aspirants; it alone is the pilgrimage to holy waters; it alone is charity; it alone is austerities. Know that there is no doubt about this". (8-9)

Bhagavan's comment: Now all your pilgrimages are over. Soham Sadhana is the last pilgrimage.

"Repeatedly say thus: I am That, the eternal, Omnipresent Reality which is Brahman. Meditating thus for a long time, whoever abides imperturbably, will become the Supreme Brahman, thereby attaining immortality". (60)

Bhagavan's comment: This is the secret of the Nath Panth. Here comes "I am That" or "That Am I"—Soham. Our system also says this. Meditate thus for a long time on the Self. You have to say repeatedly: "That I Am"—Soham. This sixtieth verse is very important.

As your mind matures, there will come a time when you should meet your Master.

In India in the nineteenth century when this was written, "Master" commonly meant an employer or a teacher of some kind. Sri Mahendranath Gupta, author of *The Gospel of Sri Ramakrishna*, was called "Master Mahasaya" by his fellow devotees. At that time both Master and Mahasaya meant a school teacher. And it is pretty much the same today. For example, I was present at a conference of school teachers in rural Bengal. Each teacher introduced himself, saying his name and adding "mahasaya" after it. ("Shuddir Bandopadhyaya Mahasaya," for example.)

The renowned master yogi, Yogiraj Shyama Charan Lahiri, was called "Lahiri Mahasaya" by his devotees and admirers, not "Guru." This is in keeping with the Nath Yogi tradition in which the teacher and taught are simply called "teacher" and "student," though usually just "friends." (See *Light of Soham*.) It reduces a lot of danger from the ego.

Whether the Master-Teacher will be a person, a book or a spiritual tradition that is encountered by the seeker is determined by the karma, samskara and the situation of the seeker's external circumstances. Sometimes a living (worthy) teacher is not to be found nearby. Either way, the Master is not groveled before and worshipped and served, but is listened to and learned from and the teaching is applied in the student's life.

Without maturation of the mind any teacher is rendered worthless by the seeker's lack of preparedness. So a true seeker eventually meets a true teacher and teaching; a partial seeker meets a partially qualified teacher; and a completely unqualified seeker meets a completely unqualified teacher or none at all. And a fake seeker finds a fake teacher. It is all determined by the qualities of the individual seeker and teacher.

This is not to say that you go in search of him or he comes in search of you. At the right time the meeting will happen. All are moving in their own ways.

In the Nath Yogi tradition it is a basic principle that the student seeks the teacher, the teacher does not seek the student. The idea is that the student must be thoroughly self-motivated and not moved or influenced by anything but the conscious desire and intention to attain higher consciousness. He is not to be "attracted" by the words or personality of the prospective teacher.

This is perfectly shown in the life and teachings of Sri Gajanana Maharaj (Gajanana Murlidhar Gupte) of Nashik found in *Light of Soham*. He prohibited his students from even speaking his name or revealing his existence. On occasion a student might tell him of an acquaintance that was interested in spiritual life. If Gajanana Maharaj intuited that the acquaintance was spiritually qualified, he might suggest that he bring him to meet him, but the meeting should be as a purely social meeting and not a spiritual event. Then things should go on from there. Some people came back just to meet Gajanana Maharaj as a person whose company and conversation they liked, and then realized he could teach them spiritually, so they asked him for teaching. He did not volunteer it. Others, of course, never came back, and that was that. The initiative always had to be on the person's part. Maharaj was just there to respond.

As I heard Yogananda say in a recorded talk: "The Masters that liberate do not want disciples" in the sense of desiring or seeking disciples. Naturally, they will accept a worthy, self-activated person. But they will not enter into a dependent parent-child kind of relationship that is so avidly sought after in both East and West as it eliminates all personal responsibility on the part of the disciple while imposing a total dependency on the guru–something a true spiritual master teacher would never tolerate or permit.

Your fitness brings you together, makes you trust him, makes him teach you the right way, also makes you follow his instructions.

The determining quality is the fitness of the aspirant, his already-developed qualities. Making the seeker fit for learning is not the work of the teacher. This is the motivating force that ensures the worthy teacher is met and recognized and trusted by the seeker. And it is the fitness of the teacher that ensures he will teach him the right way, the following of which is determined not by his persuasion or encouragement, but solely by the fitness of the seeker. It is not enough to have a qualified teacher; one must be a qualified student. Elsewhere I have written about two clueless Western "yogis" I met during my first pilgrimage to India. When they told me, "We are looking for a qualified guru," I asked them if they were qualified to be disciples. They looked shocked; then one of them said, "Probably not." But when I met them again in a few months they had been getting initiation from every "guru" they met. Nothing comes from nothing.

That is the straight way to reach God, which is to gain the fourth state.

Understanding this is absolutely essential for the aspirant. Finding the true teaching and following it to the revelation of the aspirant's own truth–the Self–is the direct way to turiya, to the entry into one's own true being. And this alone is liberation (moksha).

You will follow the way and reach your goal which is Being-Consciousness-Bliss, which is God.

That completes the picture.

8. The way shown by the Master is final, straight and making for unity. It is well-tried, natural, and free from pain. When you are following the way shown by the master, doubts will not arise; there will be no fear. Are not fear and doubt the characteristics of the ways of darkness? How can they meet you in the way of Truth shown by the Master? In this manner, the way will itself speak to you and say that it is the right one. In that way, there will be nothing more for you to do but to meet your Master and learn from him. That way will be familiar to you, as the Master and God have made it so. Before you, he had treaded the way. He has shown you the way and you are following him. To how many will you show the same way? And how many more will follow the same way later? Obviously fear and doubt have no place in the way of truth. When once you have taken a step forward you will step back. The master's help is only for the first step forward. You need not do anything for your master in order to have the way shown to you. Know him to be the messenger of God sent down to disclose the way to the fit who have become ripe by their own efforts in either or both the directions mentioned earlier. It is God who sends this godly messenger just when you are ripe.

The way shown by the Master is final, straight and making for unity.

How do you recognize a Master? Since a true Master will never teach a false way, you can determine the character of the Master by the way itself which he teaches. So let's look at the characteristics of the true teaching of a true Master.

The way is final in the sense that it leads to the final step of evolution, and is itself also a consequence of that last evolutionary step.

It is Straight in the since that it leads directly to the ultimate condition: total and permanent conscious union and identity with Brahman as the essence of all Being. And that is Unity.

All this is achieved by following the way. There is no meandering or wandering in various planes. The follower of this way never says, "I know it will be many lifetimes before I reach enlightenment." Someone saying that is unconsciously expressing his intuition that he is not following a direct path. And there is nothing but the Direct Path. The others are false and lead right back to where a person starts. And usually not older or wiser.

It is well-tried, natural, and free from pain.

Pay absolutely no attention to those who claim they have a "new" teaching or practice for a "new age." Rather, the true path is well-tried, having been known and followed for millennia beyond number. The names of those who followed it and attained the highest realization are known. Truly, it is well-tried, so we need not hesitate to travel it and reach the Goal. It is natural, because it is based on the very nature and primal makeup of the human being. Further, it is natural because it is a process that has been going on from before any world existed. And it is going on within every human being right now. It need only be told to an aspirant to set him doing consciously what he has heretofore been doing on the unconscious-subconscious level. Therefore it is also free from pain or strain since it is the first, primeval impulse of every sentient being–not just humans. But only humans have the ability to consciously begin and to carry it on. And that path is the path of the Nath Panth Yogis, the path of Soham Sadhana as outlined in *Soham Yoga: The Yoga of the Self* and *Light of Soham.*

When you are following the way shown by the master, doubts will not arise; there will be no fear. Are not fear and doubt the characteristics of the ways of darkness? How can they meet you in the way of Truth shown by the Master? In this manner, the way will itself speak to you and say that it is the right one.

You will not just have faith, you will know the way is the true way. Fear, anxiety and doubt will be things of the past, because from the first time you inwardly intone "So" as you inhale and "Ham" as you exhale and then keep doing so, both when you sit quietly and when you move around and engage in external action, you will know you have found the way. After only a few minutes of this practice for the very first time I surprised myself by spontaneously saying to myself inwardly: "Oh, I love this!" And kept on feeling that way. Having wasted over fifty years in "yoga" methods of many kinds that ultimately always turned out to be a mirage, I had found the Real Thing. Naturally my ego-mind wanted to distract me and suggested trying something else, and sometimes I did try something else for a few minutes and realized it was bogus. So I went back to Soham and stayed there. And literally enjoyed my Self. Soham Sadhana is its own proof of reality and authenticity.

In that way, there will be nothing more for you to do but to meet your Master and learn from him. That way will be familiar to you, as the Master and God have made it so.

In time you learn that God is the only guru and that your sadhana is the direct action of God in your life. The sadhana itself will teach you and open to you the inner realization and knowledge that you always had deep inside but could not access.

Before you, he had treaded the way. He has shown you the way and you are following him.

The teacher does not empower the student to walk the way, nor would he be so insane or a charlatan as to claim he has already walked the way for the student. It is a matter of simple knowledge, since the way is inherent in the student, and on the higher unconscious levels of his being he is already repeating the eternal japa of Soham. It only needs to be revealed to him in simple instruction without the mystification of secrecy or ritual.

This is why Sri Gajanana Maharaj was said to show, give or teach the way of Soham Sadhana. The matter was simple: before meeting Maharaj the student (whom Maharaj always referred to as a "friend") did not know the way, and afterward he did know the way. It was literally as simple as ABC. And from then on everything was totally up to the student. All he needed was practice and the experience gained by the practice. There was no dependence on Maharaj, for he was adamant that he was a friend, not a guru, and the friend was not a disciple. One friend wrote, "There is not even the idea of any dependence on him. Rather he makes us independent and free." This is the only true way of a true master teacher.

The author therefore continues:

To how many will you show the same way? And how many more will follow the same way later?

He who has gained experience in Soham Sadhana is qualified to teach others in the same simple way of instruction. He need not be a master yogi or liberated: only knowing and teaching the way clearly to the friend who by his own initiative and practice will set forth on the way in complete freedom and independence. No strings attached! Ever. And that friend may teach other friends in the same way and so the knowledge continues to be given in this simple manner in an unbroken exchange for generations. That is all there is to it.

Obviously fear and doubt have no place in the way of truth.
For this reason a sadhaka must be a person of stability and maturity who can trust his own experience and his own conclusions therefrom.

When once you have taken a step forward you will step back.
The idea is that you step forward to the teacher to learn, and having learned, are a student no longer, but step back and continue on your own in complete independence. You may occasionally meet with the teacher, but now as a friend and fellow-traveller on the path.

The master's help is only for the first step forward.
From then on the journey is yours alone, though the teacher remains your friend and colleague. Your contact with him will be as much or as little as you desire. But never again will you be a student—only a friend—even if you consult with him and ask him about something. His response will be to a friend and equal.

You need not do anything for your master in order to have the way shown to you.

Never does the student worship the teacher (guru puja) or give him anything (guru dakshina) in order to be instructed in sadhana. He comes empty-handed and goes empty-handed, but bears within himself the knowledge of The Way. This is the blessing of contact with a true teacher.

Know him to be the messenger of God sent down to disclose the way to the fit who have become ripe by their own efforts in either or both the directions mentioned earlier.

This is how you should think of the teacher in relation to yourself. He does indeed bear the message of God to you in the form of instruction in meditation–the way to reach union with the Divine. And that is the sum of it all.

But a real teacher will only teach the fit–those who can and will apply the sadhana he teaches. And they must realize that only their own efforts in the form of practicing meditation will "ripen" them and enable them to attain Atmajnana/Brahmajnana.

The grace we most need is our grace upon ourselves in the form of intense and prolonged sadhana practice.

It is God who sends this godly messenger just when you are ripe.

We have to be ripe to some extent as a result of our own positive samskaras before we can encounter, recognize and adopt the ways of effective sadhana imparted to us by a worthy teacher. But a worthy teacher can only help a worthy disciple. True teachers of enlightenment do not waste their time with the unworthy.

An interesting example of the messenger coming "just when you are ripe" is that of the great yogi Swami Rama, whose ashram was at the Ram Kunj in Hardwar. I was fortunate enough to know Swamiji for some years. He had been born in a village in Kashmir. One day when he was nine years old and playing in the street, an old sadhu came walking through the village. He said to the boy, "Come with me," and walked on. He followed the sadhu, and when they were at some distance from the village, the sadhu taught him a mantra and said, "Repeat this always." Then he turned and walked away. The boy never saw him again, but he followed those few words and attained real spiritual greatness.

9. Practice with faith in the period of ignorance is called Bhakti (path of Devotion); the same, with knowledge, is called Jnana (the path of Wisdom). Of the two divisions of Bhakti, the one is devotion to God with name and form, and the other is karma which is love for all. Of the two divisions of Jnana, the practice of the true way shown by the Master is called yoga and the resulting state is called Jnana (knowledge). It is natural for all to believe in something which is not seen and then to find it. Those who do not believe can never find. Therefore, the believers will gain something sometime or other and the unbelievers never gain anything. You can believe even for the simple reason that faith in God is not harmful. Thereby you can share the good effects. This world is meant only for creating faith in you. This is the purpose of creation. Have faith and you can reach God.

Practice with faith in the period of ignorance is called Bhakti (path of Devotion); the same, with knowledge, is called Jnana (the path of Wisdom).

This is a remarkable statement, one that the whole world should know, but hardly anyone does.

Swami Sivananda often said, "Devotion is not emotion." Rather, true devotion is *dedication* of oneself to God by the constant practice of sadhana. That is the sum of the whole matter.

Of the two divisions of Bhakti, the one is devotion to God with name and form, and the other is karma [yoga] which is love for all.

The first division is worship of God, singing the Names and Glories of God and–most importantly–japa of, and meditation on, the chosen Name of God. This is usually considered the whole of Bhakti, but it is not. Love of all humanity should be manifested in the practice of karma yoga in the form of benefitting others in all the ways we know and can carry out. This is true Purna [Complete] Bhakti.

> Abou Ben Adhem (may his tribe increase!)
> Awoke one night from a deep dream of peace,
> And saw, within the moonlight in his room,
> Making it rich, and like a lily in bloom,
> An angel writing in a book of gold:—
> Exceeding peace had made Ben Adhem bold,
> And to the presence in the room he said,
> "What writest thou?"—The vision raised its head,
> And with a look made of all sweet accord,

Answered, "The names of those who love the Lord."
"And is mine one?" said Abou. "Nay, not so,"
Replied the angel. Abou spoke more low,
But cheerly still; and said, "I pray thee, then,
Write me as one that loves his fellow men."

The angel wrote, and vanished. The next night
It came again with a great wakening light,
And showed the names whom love of God had blest,
And lo! Ben Adhem's name led all the rest.

Leigh Hunt

*Of the two divisions of Jnana, the practice of the true way shown
by the Master is called yoga and the resulting state is called Jnana
(knowledge).*

Sadhana is itself Jnana, for it is the Way of Wisdom and
Knowledge. And no one is a perfect Jnani until he has attained
Perfect Wisdom-Knowledge in Self-realization.

*It is natural for all to believe in something which is not seen
and then to find it.*

Every goal we set ourselves is first just an idea or imagination
in our mind. Then we apply ourselves and that goal is attained
as an actual objective reality. That is one reason why we say
"thoughts are things."

Saying we do not believe in what we do not see is not according to any reality and is utterly foolish, revealing a shallow and
cheap mind. Of course believing is not enough. We have to make

our goals objective realities. Then we can consider ourselves to have real faith.

Those who do not believe can never find.
Their life, mind and heart are all barren.

Therefore, the believers will gain something sometime or other and the unbelievers never gain anything.
Anandamayi Ma said, "The desire for God is the way to God." Desire for something is itself an inner action, a karmic force that if persisted in will bring about the desired object or result. Believing is the first step in Receiving.

You can believe even for the simple reason that faith in God is not harmful.
It will not harm anyone to believe in God. Rather it will open up in time their inner spiritual awareness and intuition if they go ahead and live and act "as though" God is real. He will manifest his existence to them.

If there is faith in something that is positive and beneficial it will come true in time as an experienced reality. Or it will lead us to something even better to believe in and actualize in our life.

Thereby you can share the good effects.
Faith does not just elevate the believer. In time it benefits all those around him–including the unbelievers.

This world is meant only for creating faith in you. This is the purpose of creation.

The very existence of the world and its marvels and miracles is a statement to us of God's existence and the possibilities open to us who believe and act accordingly.

Have faith and you can reach God.

For this is the highest benefit intended for us, the ultimate gain: Brahmajnana which by its nature is also Atmajnana.

10. Though you may not believe all that is said of God, believe at least "There is God." This seed is very potent in its growth. It is so mighty as to negate all else and fill all by itself. It is so almighty that you will not see anything besides God, not even yourself. Truly, God is all.

And THOU ART THAT.

CHAPTER FOUR–PEACE

Peace–Equanimity–Equal Mindedness

1. What is peace? Although the world persists when a man is in deep sleep, does he have any cares concerning it? His mind is tranquil and refreshed. Should his mind be in the same degree calm and refreshed even when he is face to face with the world and is active therein, then there is peace.

2. Can the mind remain so even when the world confronts us? It depends upon our estimate of the world. The mind is more excited when one's own property is plundered than when another's property is similarly plundered. Of one's own things, the loss of one thing causes greater concern than those of another. Why? Because our estimate of the things is the cause of the degree of the delight or anxiety concerning them. Therefore, should one learn to regard all equally, the mind will be extremely peaceful. Or should all things be considered as our own and highly prized, then too there is no cause for pain. Why? What will a man regret? The mind which knows that universal concern is beyond its capacity, must needs become tranquil. Also when one feels that one has no claim on anything or that everything is perishable, the mind will remain cool. Thus there will be lasting peace if

one looks on all as of the same value. Peace is dependent upon one's intellectual appraisals.

3. I shall now illustrate this. A man wakes up from a dream. His mind is happy or troubled according to his opinion of the things seen in the dream. But on waking, his mind remains unaffected by all the happenings in the dream; it remains the same. Why? Because, only now his mind has learned to value all the matters of the dream equally. He is not sorry for the cessation of the dream. Why? He is convinced that the dream is not everlasting and must end on waking. In the same manner, should a man be convinced that he cannot but wake up sometime from the long dream of the world, his mind will be unchanging. It is the state of freshness. This is the state of Peace.

4. This is not to say that his relation with the world will cease. Now only peace and freshness of the mind are his. His actions cannot but vary according to circumstances. The only change in him after the mind has become peaceful is this: his mind has known the truth and become unattached; therefore, it rests in peace. His actions though changeful will always be impartial. But the actions of others are changing and cannot be impartial. Thus, the coolness of the mind produces enormous good not only to himself but also to the world at large. Peace shows the way to right conduct.

5. A man walks with a lighted lamp in his hand. Can there be any hostility between the light and the ups and downs on the way? There cannot be. But light and darkness cannot be together. The light chases away darkness, it discloses the ups and downs on the way and makes the man walk carefully, whether

he moves up, down, or sideways. It removes the cause of vain complaints, such as, "That snag hurt my foot" or "This hollow made me slip." Similarly, after peace is gained, the state of peace makes the man neither hate nor antagonize the world. Rather it dispels the darkness which conceals from our view the true nature of the world and its snags. In the absence of the light of Peace which enables people to adjust themselves to varying circumstances, they condemn the world as full of misery, as they would complain of the snags on the road. Therefore a man who has gained the utmost peace after knowing the whole world as a complicated dream should not be considered either unrelated to the world or unconcerned with its activities; he alone stands in effective concord with it; only he is competent to be a man of action. Thus Peace is that which regulates one's duties.

6. The concern of a man of Peace in the actions of the world lies in rectifying them. Should he feel fear before this world, what hope of reformation can there be, especially from those who esteem it and want to possess it? They are in the grip of selfishness, blind to impartiality. To guide the blind on the way or treat the blindness of the eye, one's eyesight must itself be good. Similarly, it is for him to reform the world who has already discerned his unchanging nature from the changeful nature of the world and become peaceful. These cannot help serving the world. Why? Can anyone be so hard-hearted as not to lift up a child when it slips and falls? So also for the wise ones who can rightly appraise the troubles of the world and help the people. Because he has already withdrawn himself from the mind and body the sage feels no concern under the strain of service to the

world, just as the life principle does not suffer even when loaded carts pass over the corpse it has left behind (by itself). He will not shrink from work or trouble. Only truly realized peace can bestow such courage and coolness.

7. To all appearances, Peace will look poor and quite weak. But in effect, it beats all. In tenacity and courage, it surpasses all. After all, success depends on these qualities. Even if Mount Meru should topple over, the incident will hardly produce a gentle smile in the man of peace, or it will leave him unmoved. This state is helpful both for worldly and spiritual matters. True happiness in the world is his, and that happiness comes out of release from bondage. Peace means doing good to any one in any manner.

8. The obstacles to peace are several. They are meant to prove the man. When they confront us we should be wide awake and keep the delicate flower of the mind distant from even their shadows. If the flower of the mind be crushed, it will lose its fragrance, freshness and color; it will neither be useful to you, nor can it be presented to others, nor offered to God. Know that your mind is more delicate than even a blossom. By means of a peaceful mind, all your duties to yourself, to others and to God must be discharged. Let it release the same freshness throughout. All blessings for the mind are contained in Peace.

9. Unremittingly worship the God of your Self with the flower of your mind. Let the children of the mental modes watch this worship. Gradually they will learn to cast away their childish pranks and desire to delight like yourself. As they watch your Peace, they will themselves recoil from their vagaries. Continue

the worship patiently. Be not led away by the vagaries of the mind. On the contrary, they should become peaceful by your peace. All must get peace.

10. I shall finish in one word: The essence of all the Vedas is "Peace."

Commentary

1. What is peace? Although the world persists when a man is in deep sleep, does he have any cares concerning it? His mind is tranquil and refreshed. Should his mind be in the same degree calm and refreshed even when he is face to face with the world and is active therein, then there is peace.

The state of deep sleep while yet awake is the highest form of Yoga Nidra–Yogic Sleep. This state arises in deep meditation and by the continual practice of meditation comes to pervade our waking hours even when we are engaged in activity and interaction with the world around us. And by meditation I mean meditation on Soham–not the pondering of the meaning "I Am That," but an entering into the experience of that fact through Soham Yoga Sadhana: intoning *So* throughout every inhalation and *Ham* ["Hum"] throughout every exhalation.

This is the way to true and lasting peace.

2. Can the mind remain so even when the world confronts us? It depends upon our estimate of the world. The mind is more excited when one's own property is plundered than when another's property is similarly plundered. Of one's own things, the loss of one thing causes greater concern than those of another. Why? Because our estimate of the things is the cause of the degree of the delight or anxiety concerning them. Therefore, should one learn to regard all equally, the mind will be extremely peaceful. Or should all things be considered as our own and highly prized, then too there is no cause for pain. Why? What will a man regret? The mind which knows that universal concern is beyond its capacity, must needs become tranquil. Also when one feels that one has no claim on anything or that everything is perishable, the mind will remain cool. Thus there will be lasting peace if one looks on all as of the same value. Peace is dependent upon one's intellectual appraisals.

Can the mind remain so even when the world confronts us? It depends upon our estimate of the world.

Our opinion of the nature of the world determines the state of our mind when we experience it. As Sri Ramakrishna said, "The mind is everything." Our reaction to the world, including motion pictures and the words of others, is according to our view of the world and those within it. And in certain aspects our view of the world determines its reaction on us rather than its innate character.

I am reminded of the time a young girl who traveled with Anandamayi Ma got it into her head that she was not being treated as she should be and went with her parents (whom I knew) to complain to Ma. She laid out her case in great detail and waited with her parents for Ma to apologize or say she would see that the girl was treated better in the future. But Ma quite firmly said to the three of them: "Since you have chosen to see it this way: then it *is* this way." All three of them cried, of course, as weak, spiteful people always do, but Ma remained firm.

My father-mother-teacher Aunt Faye Mitchell once read me this poem:

Don't be a Croaker

Once by the edge of a pleasant pool,
Under the bank where it was dark and cool,
Where the bushes over the water hung,
And the grasses nodded and the rushes swung.
Just where the brook flowed out of the bog,
There lived a gouty and mean old frog,
Who'd sit all day in the mud and soak,
And do just nothing but croak and croak.

Till a blackbird whistled, "I say you know—
What's the matter down there below?
Are you in pain, or sorrow or what?"
And the frog answered, "Mine is a gruesome lot—
Nothing but dirt and mud and slime
For me to look at all the live-long time.
'Tis a dismal world," he sadly spoke,
And voiced his woes with a mournful croak.

"But you're looking down," the blackbird said,
"Look at the blossoms overhead,
Look at the beautiful summer skies,

Look at the bees and the butterflies.
Look up, old fellow, why bless my soul,
You're looking down in a muskrat's hole."
But still with gurgling sob and choke
The frog continued to croak and croak.

But a wise old turtle–who boarded near–
Said to the blackbird, "Friend, see here,
Don't waste your tears on him, for he
Is miserable 'cause he wants to be–
He is one of the kind that won't be glad,
And it makes him happy to think he's sad,
I'll tell you something–and it's no joke–
Don't waste your pity on those who croak."

Ma said it briefer, but the truth is the same.

The mind is more excited when one's own property is plundered than when another's property is similarly plundered. Of one's own things, the loss of one thing causes greater concern than those of another. Why? Because our estimate of the things is the cause of the degree of the delight or anxiety concerning them. Therefore, should one learn to regard all equally, the mind will be extremely peaceful. Or should all things be considered as our own and highly prized, then too there is no cause for pain. Why? What will a man regret? The mind which knows that universal concern is beyond its capacity, must needs become tranquil. Also when one feels that one has no claim on anything or that everything is perishable, the mind will remain cool. *Thus there will be lasting peace if one looks on all as of the same value. Peace is dependent upon one's intellectual appraisals.*

We should neither have too high or too low a regard for anything. They are simply waves in the ocean of creative energy that surrounds us and of which even our bodies are a part. In one viewpoint we should realize that nothing really has intrinsic value, being just an appearance. At the same time we should consider everything of infinite value because it is a manifestation of the Infinite. So we should simultaneously disregard and value all things—and all people as well. This is the detachment the Bhagavad Gita urges upon us throughout. Viveka and vairagya are the divine keys to the world of peace.

3. I shall now illustrate this. A man wakes up from a dream. His mind is happy or troubled according to his opinion of the things seen in the dream. But on waking, his mind remains unaffected by all the happenings in the dream; it remains the same. Why? Because, only now his mind has learned to value all the matters of the dream equally. He is not sorry for the cessation of the dream. Why? He is convinced that the dream is not everlasting and must end on waking. In the same manner, should a man be convinced that he cannot but wake up sometime from the long dream of the world, his mind will be unchanging. It is the state of freshness. This is the state of Peace.

I shall now illustrate this. A man wakes up from a dream. His mind is happy or troubled according to his opinion of the things seen in the dream. But on waking, his mind remains unaffected by all the happenings in the dream; it remains the same. Why?

Because, only now his mind has learned to value all the matters of the dream equally.

And there is a bit more. His waking perspective enables him to see that the dream had no basis even in the relative reality such as this world is. It really was "all in his head" and insubstantial on every level. It existed only as a mirage, an hallucination, even. Therefore:

He is not sorry for the cessation of the dream. Why? He is convinced that the dream is not everlasting and must end on waking. In the same manner, should a man be convinced that he cannot but wake up sometime from the long dream of the world, his mind will be unchanging. It is the state of freshness. This is the state of Peace.

Now this requires an intense act of will, of resistance to our lower mind which naturally believes all the illusions and even may strive itself to maintain them, mistaking them for reality. This also demands a profound degree of faith because it goes completely against all our experiences—what we have always thought we knew as real or true. So to attain that peace of will is not a small thing. Actually it is spiritually heroic.

Peace comes at a price, and to the conditioned mind it is an impossible and even undesirable price. We should never be quick to condemn or disapprove of those who adamantly or even emotionally resist the highest truth of things since it does not tally with their lifelong experience. To consider that all "things" are illusions is to confess oneself and nearly everyone else in the world as deluded! This is very difficult for the conditioned, logical mind, what to say of the ego that has been in charge of everything in our life for so long and who considers the acceptance of Advaitic principles and acting upon them as its death sentence–which it is!

4. This is not to say that his relation with the world will cease. Now only peace and freshness of the mind are his. His actions cannot but vary according to circumstances. The only change in him after the mind has become peaceful is this: his mind has known the truth and become unattached; therefore, it rests in peace. His actions though changeful will always be impartial. But the actions of others are changing and cannot be impartial. Thus, the coolness of the mind produces enormous good not only to himself but also to the world at large. Peace shows the way to right conduct.

This is not to say that his relation with the world will cease.

But to the deluded and uncomprehending ego-mind it will seem inevitable. And it actually is, since understanding the nature of something must change our idea of and about it. So we can sympathize with those who resist these truths, for they are only liberating to those who see truly and accept them as they are: bedrock truth.

The awakened individual's relation to the world is drastically altered in his mind and later conduct. To the truly insightful person this is a blessed and freeing event, but to another, outside observer it can be seen as imprisonment or destruction. So the sadhaka must always cultivate an understanding and tolerant attitude toward those who are intolerant and resistant to what we know as blessed truths.

Now only peace and freshness of the mind are his.

But often only after a great struggle within himself and with those who point him to the freedom he considers imaginary and enslaving.

It is not easy to be a child, because adults universally forget what it was like for them to be a child. In fact, even when they remember their own childhood they do so while projecting into their memories their adult attitudes and outlook on the events–which of course they did not have at the time–and therefore do not at all remember the inner, emotional and personal experience of their childhood. Instead they are impatient with children whom they consider unreasonable and difficult when they are themselves the unreasonable and difficult ones. Consequently they demand that a child think and act like an adult: an impossibility. So conflict and pain result over and over from generation to generation.

When I was a child it was a blessed relief to meet an adult who remembered what it was like to be a child and therefore treated me with insight and understanding. So I am aware that it is essential that spiritual adults remember when they were spiritual children and treat those they meet with understanding and help them to their own gaining of understanding.

His actions cannot but vary according to circumstances.

This is a trait of a broad, multifaceted mind. In this statement it means a person whose mind has been expanded, not just intellectually but through the development of the higher mode of thought we call intuition, which is really the *knowing* of the buddhi (intellect) rather than the simple manas (mind). It also indicates a sensitivity to other people and a clear understanding of circumstances that has arisen from insight rather than mere reasoning or past experience.

The Bhagavad Gita (18:22) says that a person of darkened and dull (tamasic) intellect thinks there is only one side to anything; that a single thing is the whole. These are the people that consider there is only one way to deal with a situation, for example, and who also think that one idea or principle is the whole perspective. In religion, for example, they choose some idea or action and say that idea or action is all there is to some philosophical view or virtuous action. "All you need do…" is their preface to a single idea or deed they consider is the whole of truth or right conduct.

The only change in him after the mind has become peaceful is this: his mind has known the truth and become unattached; therefore, it rests in peace.

Genuine knowing produces these changes in the individual's mind and personality. Detachment is a quality of satisfaction and fulfillment. "When a man has found delight and satisfaction and peace in the Atman, then he is no longer obliged to perform any kind of action. He has nothing to gain in this world by action, and nothing to lose by refraining from action. He is independent of everybody and everything" (Bhagavad Gita 3:17-18). Therefore he is totally at peace in the Self.

His actions though changeful will always be impartial. But the actions of others are changing and cannot be impartial.

The enlightened man never looks at things from the perspective of the lower ego-mind, for that has been transmuted into the pure light (shuddha sattwa) of the buddhi established in the Self. He sees all things in a still mind like a flawless mirror. And his actions proceed from this perspective.

Thus, the coolness of the mind produces enormous good not only to himself but also to the world at large.

To have a cool mind means that the individual does not stir up either himself or others. He sees and approaches all things with equanimity, with clarity and calmness of mind. In this way he benefits both himself and the world (including people) that he encounters.

"He who agitates not the world, and whom the world agitates not, who is freed from joy, envy, fear and distress–he is dear to me" (Bhagavad Gita 12:15).

"Like the ocean, which becomes filled yet remains unmoved and stands still as the waters enter it, he whom all desires enter and who remains unmoved attains peace–not so the man who is full of desire. He who abandons all desires attains peace, acts free from longing, indifferent to possessions and free from egotism" (Bhagavad Gita 2:70-71).

Peace shows the way to right conduct.

This is because peace is also clarity of mind, as just said. As a mirror reflects the objects before it, so the steady and clear mind imparts to us an accurate and steady view of the world, and our reactions will also be accurate and steady, for the conduct of a person mirrors his mind.

*5. A man walks with a lighted lamp in his hand. Can there be
any hostility between the light and the ups and downs on the way?
There cannot be.*

There is no hostility or conflict between the ups and down
on a path because they are only modifications in a single thing:
the earth. So when there is unity of mind and everything is seen
as one, the light of the individual's mind simply reflects and
does not react to differences, but remains objective. There is no
permanent peace outside of unity of subject and object, of the
seer and the seen.

*But light and darkness cannot be together. The light chases away
darkness, it discloses the ups and downs on the way and makes the
man walk carefully, whether he moves up, down, or sideways. It
removes the cause of vain complaints, such as, "That snag hurt my
foot" or "This hollow made me slip." Similarly, after peace is gained,
the state of peace makes the man neither hate nor antagonize the
world. Rather it dispels the darkness which conceals from our view
the true nature of the world and its snags.*

Illumination of the buddhi is the secret of this state. This is
a wonderful description of the enlightened mind and should be
read over carefully more than once.

*In the absence of the light of Peace which enables people to adjust
themselves to varying circumstances, they condemn the world as full
of misery, as they would complain of the snags on the road.*

Again we see the fundamental truth of Sri Ramakrishna's
statement that the mind is everything. The way we see the world

is the way our mind is. In a sense we see our mind, ourself, we when we look out at the world. If the window is dirty or fogged up we see the world as obscure, and if the window is clean we see the world as clear. If a mirror is bent, we see the world as bent. If it is straight, we see the world as straight. I knew a woman whose little boy came in from playing. When he passed the mirror he saw his smudgy and dusty face as the result of his playing. Later he washed face and when he passed the mirror stopped and said: "We must have a new mirror!"

The change we need is a change inside.

Therefore a man who has gained the utmost peace after knowing the whole world as a complicated dream, should not be considered either unrelated to the world or unconcerned with its activities; he alone stands in effective concord with it; only he is competent to be a man of action. Thus Peace is that which regulates one's duties.

This is a remarkable insight. The jnani does not engage in the usual unthinking interaction with the world that characterizes an ordinary person, yet he is not truly aloof or indifferent. Rather, he is cool of mind and only engages himself when it is consonant with absolute wisdom. He sees all aspects of a situation and determines whether action or inaction is the most effective toward the state of liberation. He never foolishly thinks he has attained the All, and is never unaware of the need for caution and care at all times as he wends his way through this world, putting his steps only where they will move him upward. He is fearless, but never careless or unheeding. He sees with both the eyes of the body and the eyes of the mind simultaneously. His every action is a movement toward enlightenment.

6. The concern of a man of Peace in the actions of the world lies in rectifying them.

Correction often comes in the form of healing, and it takes a high level of consciousness to truly heal right to the roots of the problem—otherwise it recurs in the future. Such healing is total purification, a dispelling of all that blocks or is a potentially harmful factor. In other words, healing has to go to the root in its effect. Only a person who has plumbed the depths and the heights of his own person and its constituents can effect permanent healing or correction. He must himself be free of any element that needs correcting or healing. Otherwise even his good will is useless. It is an absolute principle: "Physician, heal thyself" (Luke 4:23). Yogananda often said, "Save yourself and you will save thousands." Earlier Saint Seraphim of Sarov said: "Acquire the Spirit of Peace and thousands around you will be saved."

First we make ourselves right, then our very thought or presence can make situations and others right. I have read of great souls who merely walked through troubled or negative places and left them peaceful and pure. Only a look from such a highly evolved person can work miracles. The shadow of Saint Peter the Apostle cured the sick. "They brought forth the sick into the streets, and laid them on beds and couches, that at the least the shadow of Peter passing by might overshadow some of them. There came also a multitude out of the cities round about unto

Jerusalem, bringing sick folks, and them which were vexed with unclean spirits: and they were healed every one" (Acts 5:15-16). Cloths touched to the body of Saint Paul exorcised evil spirits. "And God wrought special miracles by the hands of Paul: So that from his body were brought unto the sick handkerchiefs or aprons, and the diseases departed from them, and the evil spirits went out of them" (Acts 19:11-12).

This can only happen when a person has become transmuted in his entire being. And as said before, it is yoga sadhana alone that works this divine alchemy.

Should he feel fear before this world, what hope of reformation can there be, especially from those who esteem it and want to possess it?

No one can uplift the world who is any way intimidated by the world and feels the slightest fear or hesitation in speaking the truth about it or exposing its manifold flaws. There is no hope of reforming any aspect of the world or any of those living in the world by someone who values and seeks after anything which is "of the earth earthly." Nor can those who value and seek after anything of this world be reformed by anyone, no matter how great the would-be reformer might be. For as Abraham said to the man in Jesus' parable of the beggar Lazarus, "Between us and you there is a great gulf fixed: so that they which would pass from hence to you cannot; neither can they pass to us, that would come from thence" (Luke 16:26). The inner, spiritual separation is great and impassable, though it is invisible to earthly eyes. The wise know this and never attempt to enlighten or change those who love and desire this world or anything in it. "Ephraim is joined to idols: let him alone" (Hosea 4:17). In other words, as the old adage says: "Never try to teach a pig to sing. It only wastes your time and annoys the pig." This may seem "negative" to those who pretty-think all the time to cover up their own negativity, but the author continues, describing the hopeless cases:

They are in the grip of selfishness, blind to impartiality.

Such people have neither viveka nor vairagya, neither discrimination nor detachment, regarding the world and its ways. They like what they see, and they see what they like. Therefore the author says further:

To guide the blind on the way or treat the blindness of the eye, one's eyesight must itself be good.

"Abiding in the midst of ignorance, wise in their own esteem, thinking themselves to be learned, fools, afflicted with troubles, go about like blind men led by one who is himself blind" (Mundaka Upanishad 1.2.8). Ignorant people like to be guided by those that are equally ignorant, for their attitudes and outlook will be the same. The words and sayings of the wise conflict with theirs, so they avoid the wise. But there is no hope for the blind who do not listen to and be led by those who see, and see clearly. Therefore those who would lead others must know the way, having themselves traveled it before.

The religious and spiritual world is filled with blind and half-blind leaders of those blind and half-blind like themselves.

They get along very well and are contented with one another. A false seeker finds a false teacher and is satisfied. This is the way it has always been and will continue to be so.

Similarly, it is for him to reform the world who has already discerned his unchanging nature from the changeful nature of the world and become peaceful.

Only a person who is fully established in the knowledge of the Self is qualified to assist others in their journey toward enlightenment in the Self. Even a qualified teacher can do nothing with those who are not qualified students, nor can they benefit from anyone else but a qualified teacher. So the worthy teacher only teaches worthy aspirants. The best example of both worthy teacher and students I know is that of Sri Gajanana Maharaj of Nashik whose life and teachings can be found in the book *Light of Soham*.

One who has known the Self knows well what is not the Self, but the world and its ways in no way unsettles or saddens him. Rather, he is glad he has awakened into reality and knows the difference between the unreal and the Real. Truly he is at peace within himself and with all around him.

These cannot help serving the world. Why? Can anyone be so hard-hearted as not to lift up a child when it slips and falls? So also for the wise ones who can rightly appraise the troubles of the world and help the people.

It is natural and spontaneous for a person of true Self-realization to help those who are ready to turn from pursuit of the world and seek their own Self-realization. But he is not "innocent" or naive, and knows that most people do not want true Brahmajnana/Atmajnana. And he not only rightly appraises the troubles of the world, he rightly appraises the inner disposition of those in the world. He can distinguish between those whom he can help and those he cannot help because they do not want deliverance from samsara and its miseries, since they esteem and desire to possess the world. He takes from the troubles of the world only those who wish to be freed from them.

There is a story of a boy scout who tried to follow the motto of Do A Good Turn Daily. One time a boy came to his scout meeting all bruised and scratched and with his clothes torn. When the scoutmaster asked him what had happened, he said, "I helped an old lady across the street, and she did this to me." "But, why would she do that?" demanded the scoutmaster. "She didn't want to go across the street," was the reply. There are those who feel at home in the world, and those that know they are strangers here. The wise know that they are just passing through this world to higher realms of consciousness. So they seek to gain higher consciousness so they will pass beyond this world and enter those realms.

The first time I consulted Dr. Josef Lenninger, the greatest medical practitioner I have ever known, he sat in silence a bit and then looked at me and said, "Why did you come to this lousy world? This is no place for you." The truth is, none of us really belong here. It is just a rung on a ladder of evolutionary experience which we must step up from and keep on moving up until we can step off the ladder itself and into Freedom.

But the problem is that we are immortal, eternal spirit-selves encased in the energy forms that are our physical, astral and causal bodies with which we mistakenly identify. All these bodies are vehicles for us, but they are not us. But because of so many incarnations in the lower worlds we identify with our prisons and not with the prisoner within. But a worthy teacher can show us the way to freedom. He turns the true seekers into true finders.

Because he has already withdrawn himself from the mind and body the sage feels no concern under the strain of service to the world, just as the life principle does not suffer even when loaded carts pass over the corpse it has left behind (by itself). He will not shrink from work or trouble. Only truly realized peace can bestow such courage and coolness.

It is often amazing the amount of work that can be done by a person of spiritual realization. Many renowned saints have astounded observers by their accomplishments. This is because they live in the Source of life energies. Many never slept, or only very little. Saint John Maximovitch slept only thirty minutes or less in a day. Anandamayi Ma never slept, though she would lie down quietly (mostly to avoid being bothered by people). Saint John Bosco was another living dynamo. It is thought that Ramana Maharshi never slept. Waking, sleep and dreamless sleep are states of the body and mind. Those who have realized themselves as beyond these three are living always in the fourth level of pure consciousness known as turiya. So they are in no "state" at all, but in That which is beyond and yet pervades all such states. It cannot be intellectually defined or described. They really are not anything, and at the same time everything. Instead of trying to understand them we should strive to become the same as they are, for this is our true nature as much as theirs. I knew a yogi that was traveling outside India. When he took a ferry from an island to the mainland, a little girl came up to him, looking at his clothing and general appearance, and asked him: "What are you supposed to be?" He smiled and quietly answered, "Oh, just what I am supposed to be." Perhaps that is why on the three-hour ferry journey a line of seagulls flew opposite the window of his stateroom, watching him intently. I know. I was there.

7. To all appearances, Peace will look poor and quite weak. But in effect, it beats [conquers; overcomes] all. In tenacity and courage, it surpasses all. After all, success depends on these qualities.

To brutish and simplistic minds peace and gentleness have always been mocked and despised as weakness and even stupidity by evil and violent bullies, what to speak of aggressive egotists. But the truly peaceful person is both confident and endurant, and therefore courageous. Such a person is also tenacious and perseverant and therefore succeeds over even great odds, for as the author says, success depends on these qualities. And peace is the source of them all.

Even if Mount Meru should topple over, the incident will hardly produce a gentle smile in the man of peace, or it will leave him unmoved.

"Unshaken amidst the crash of falling worlds" is how Yogananda described this state.

This state is helpful both for worldly and spiritual matters.
The logic of this is so apparent that there is no real need for comment except to note that peace prevails in both worldly and spiritual matters because, as Sri Ramakrishna often said, "If you can weigh salt you can weigh sugar." That is, if you have intelligence, will power and endurance in secular endeavors you will succeed, and if you have those qualities in spiritual life you will succeed equally well.

At the root of this statement is also the absolute need to live both worldly and spiritual life to the best of your abilities, for both lives are means for the production of the karmas and samskaras that lead to the highest realization when the sadhaka applies himself equally well in both, for the One is itself at the root of all things and situations as their essential being, just as it is at the root of us as our essential being.

True happiness in the world is his, and that happiness comes out of release from bondage.
Moksha is only attained by the fully competent in all aspects of their existence. And here, too, only the yogi is fully able to demonstrate this. When I was a feeble aspirant practicing fake yoga, this idea would have repulsed me as hypocritical and materialistic because I was, like all falsely "spiritual" people, incompetent in both my inner and outer lives. But when I became a real yogi, to my own astonishment I found that the

author is right, and I was able to live both lives in contentment and assurance. This is why the yogi is abhaya–without fear or anxiety. Those not in this state are not yogis, however much they may mistakenly think they are. "Otherworldly" people are not fit for any world. And those who are not Here and Now will never reach the Infinite There.

Peace means doing good to any one in any manner.

I believe that a better way to express this would be: The state of Peace manifests as doing good to anyone in any manner. It necessarily implies that good is done to every one in the orbit of a person's life–not just a chosen number. So a true person of peace will always live in this manner and act in this way to all without exception. In India they say that a rose and sandalwood both emanate sweet perfume when crushed underfoot; and in the same way the truly good only give good in return for evil. This, too, would be an aspect of this peace.

8. The obstacles to peace are several. They are meant to prove the man.

In the world of samsara, the realm of duality, there is always opposition of the negative to the positive. Furthermore, there are several obstacles to peace–though the author does not list them. But we will encounter them inevitably as we move toward the state (bhava) of true peace. And if we recognize and meet them in the right, dharmic manner they shall make us strong and steadfast, unwavering in our journey to Freedom, just as powerful wind causes the roots of a tree to grow deeper and stronger.

We must not forget the opening words of the Bhagavad Gita: *Dharmakshetre Kurukshetre Samaveta Yuyutsavah*: "On the field of Dharma, Kurukshetra, assembled together, desiring to fight...." The place of dharma is the place where there is willing and united struggle of good against evil, a struggle destined to end in the victory of good over evil and the banishment of evil. No fight–no victory.

The heart, mind and life of the sadhaka is the field of battle in which we fight. It is significant that the Field of Dharma is called the Field of the Kurus–the evil ones that were opposing the good. Both the world around and within us are in the possession-control of ignorance and negativity symbolized by the Kurus. We must reverse this condition through continuous and intense inner and outer processes of purification. We must place the Pandavas (the original owners of the field) on their rightful throne. The five Pandava brothers represent the positive conditions of the five elements that comprise our five bodies and five senses as well as the entire range of relative existence. All of our being must be engaged in the process of spiritual empowerment and victory. And this process is both external and internal, encompassing our outer and inner life. This alone brings Freedom.

When they confront us we should be wide awake and keep the delicate flower of the mind distant from even their shadows.
Before looking at the whole sentence, there are two very important points I would like to consider that are themselves to be kept in mind at all times by the sadhaka.

First, we must at all time be "wide awake"–not just somewhat or even to a great extent, but totally awake and alert. Otherwise we may not notice something that is potentially to our benefit or our harm. Nothing must be considered not worth examining. We must in a sense be "all eyes" at all times, because subtle negativity or neglect can be more deadly than very overt negativity or neglect. To not be fully awake is to not be fully alive.

Second, that the mind is delicate by virtue of its subtlety, that its cultivation must not be neglected, and it must be protected at all times. This is done by shielding it from all that is negative and detrimental, and most of all by keeping it strong and resistant. The mind of a yogi by its refinement and multifaceted development is like a flower in its unfoldment and must be looked after as a flower is tended and sheltered. There is no place in the sadhaka's life for brashness and foolish confidence that will render it vulnerable through failure to be vigilant and cautious.

The obstacles to our Self-realization are literally deadly, as I have already said. Those inexperienced in the yoga life almost never have a right response to those things, but think they are of little or no consequence because they do not realize the great harm they can produce in the long run. This is especially true when the obstacles are the qualities or elements of their own mind and personality–their samskaras. It is always necessary to keep the mind and heart "distant even from their shadows." Not even a hint of delusion and illusion should be allow to remain in us.

If the flower of the mind be crushed, it will lose its fragrance, freshness and color; it will neither be useful to you, nor can it be presented to others, nor offered to God.

This is truly being lost and negated.

Know that your mind is more delicate than even a blossom.

I should say here that when the word "mind" is used the usual word is manas: the sensory mind; the perceiving faculty that receives the messages of the senses. But in this book it includes the buddhi: intellect; intelligence; understanding; reason; the thinking mind; the higher mind, which is the seat of wisdom; the discriminating faculty.

The entire subtle energy field of the manas and buddhi together is subtle and delicate, even fragile in some situations. The mind, like the body, can take a lot of abuse–even damage– and survive. But it will be inhibited or limited in its functioning, so the wise person protects and shields it in various ways, especially in what it becomes exposed (and therefore vulnerable) to.

A major factor is diet, for just as the physical substance of food becomes assimilated into our physical body, the subtler energies become united to our inner levels, including our mind. The observant yogi will discover that the diet of the physical body is also the diet of the mind, that whatever is eaten physically will have an effect mentally. Here are some statements about the nature and effect of food that are found in the upanishads.

"From food [has arisen] vital vigor, austerity and works" (Prashna Upanishad 6.4). Obviously the kind of food we eat will determine the quality of our sadhana (austerity: tapasya).

"By food, indeed, do all the vital breaths [pranas, life forces] become great" (Taittiriya Upanishad 1.5.4).

"A person consists of the essence of food" (Taittiriya Upanishad 2.1.1). So we are what we eat.

"From food, verily, are produced whatsoever creatures dwell on the earth. Moreover, by food alone they live…. From food are beings born. When born they grow up by food…. Verily, different from and within that which consists of the essence of food is the self that consists of life. By that this is filled. This, verily, has the form of a person. According to that one's personal form is this one with the form of a person." (Taittiriya Upanishad 2.2.1). The spiritual (astral/causal) body is drawn exclusively from food, so diet is crucial in spiritual development.

"Food when eaten becomes threefold, its coarsest portion becomes the faeces; its middle (portion) flesh, and its subtlest (portion) mind. Water when drunk becomes threefold, its coarsest portion becomes the urine; its middle (portion) the blood, its subtlest (portion) the breath…. Thus, my dear, mind consists of food, and breath consists of water…." (Chandogya Upanishad 6.5.1-2, 4).

"That which is the subtlest part of curds rises, when they are churned and becomes butter. In the same manner that which is the subtlest part of the food that is eaten rises and becomes mind. Thus the mind consists of food" (Chandogya Upanishad 6.6.1, 2,5; the same is confirmed in 6.6.1-5).

"When food is pure, the mind is pure, When the mind is pure, memory becomes firm. When memory [smriti–memory of our eternal spirit-Self] remains firm, there is release from all

CHAPTER FOUR-PEACE

knots of the heart. To such a one who has his stains wiped away, Bhagavan Sanatkumara shows the further shore of darkness" (Chandogya Upanishad 7.26.2).

"In food everything rests, whatsoever breathes and what does not" (Brihadaranyaka Upanishad 1.5.1).

By means of a peaceful mind, all your duties to yourself, to others and to God must be discharged. Let it release the same freshness throughout. All blessings for the mind are contained in Peace.

This will always be true of the yogi especially. "For the undisciplined there is no wisdom, no meditation. For him who does not meditate there is no peace or happiness" (Bhagavad Gita 2:66).

9. Unremittingly worship the God of your Self with the flower of your mind.

Worship, upasana, means "sitting near" or "drawing near." This includes meditation, which is a process centered in the mind. We cannot sit in meditation all the day, so how can it be done unremittingly–all the time? By the simple practice of japa: repetition of a mantra. Sri M. P. Pandit wrote the following regarding the practice of japa.

"What is Japa? What is its rationale? What is its process? Japa is the repetition of a Mantra, a potent syllable or syllables, a word or a combination of words, done with the object of realizing the truth embodied in the Mantra [which] has the necessary power within it. And by constant repetition under proper conditions the power can be evoked into operation. The vibrations set up

94

each time the Mantra is repeated go to create, in the subtler atmosphere, the conditions that induce the fulfillment of the object in view. The Divine Name, for instance, has the potency to stamp and mould the consciousness which repeats it into the nature of the Divinity for which the Name stands and prepare it for the reception of the gathering Revelation of the Godhead.

"At the basis of the Science of Japa is the ancient perception of sages all over the world that Creation proceeds from Sound. The universe has issued out of Nada Brahman, Brahman as Sound. This perception of the inherent power of sound, shabda, was applied with remarkable success by Indian adepts in Yoga who have reduced their knowledge and experience to an exact Science. When repeated for a long time, the Mantra goes on creating vibrations which press upon the layers of the inner consciousness till one day there comes a sudden opening and the Truth ensouled in the Mantra reveals itself."

Let the children of the mental modes watch this worship.

Let all the aspects of the mind, which include the inner senses and faculties as well as the moods and actual thoughts, become absorbed in the experiencing of the inner mental repetitions (japa) of the mantra.

What mantra is best for this japa? Sri Ramana Maharshi, who often recommended *Ellam Ondre*, said: "Since the Self is the reality of all the gods, the meditation on the Self which is oneself is the greatest of all meditations. All other meditations are included in this. It is for gaining this that the other meditations are prescribed. So, if this is gained, the others are not necessary. Knowing one's Self is knowing God. Without knowing one's Self that meditates, imagining that there is a deity which is different and meditating on it, is compared by the great ones to the act of measuring with one's foot one's own shadow, and to the search for a trivial conch [shell] after throwing away a priceless gem that is already in one's possession" (*Collected Works*, section 28).

The perfect mantra is Soham, for Sri Ramana Maharshi was asked: "What is the purport of the teaching that one should meditate, through the 'I am That' [Soham] thought, on the truth that one is not different from the self-luminous Reality that shines like a flame?"

Bhagavan replied: "The purport of teaching that one should meditate with the 'I am That' thought is this: sah-aham: So'ham; sah the supreme Self, aham the Self that is manifest as 'I.' If one meditates for a long time, without disturbance, on the Self ceaselessly, with the 'So'ham–I am That' thought which is the technique of reflection on the Self, the darkness of ignorance which is in the heart and all the impediments which are but the effects of ignorance will be removed, and the plenary wisdom will be gained.... The body is the temple; the jiva is God (Shiva). If one worships him with the 'So'ham–I am That' thought, one will gain release" (*Collected Works* [Section] 29).

Sri Ramana Maharshi was shown the Sanskrit text of *Devikallotara Jnanachara Vichara Padalam* (A Study of the Exposition of Supreme Wisdom and Conduct to Goddess Ishwari by Lord Shiva) written on palm leaves. He said that this writing was very, very important, and himself translated it into Tamil with his commentary. Sri T. K. Jayaram then translated it into English, including the following:

[Shiva said to Parvati:] The means by which this mind, which is restless and moves about quicker than the wind, can be brought under control, is indeed the means to obtain liberation; is indeed what is good for those who seek permanent Reality; it itself is pure Consciousness and the state of firmness; moreover, it alone is the righteous duty to be followed by discerning aspirants; it alone is the pilgrimage to holy waters; it alone is charity; it alone is austerities. Know that there is no doubt about this. (8-9)

Bhagavan's comment: Now all your pilgrimages are over. Soham Sadhana is the last pilgrimage.

Repeatedly say thus: I am That, the eternal, Omnipresent Reality which is Brahman. Meditating thus for a long time, whoever abides imperturbably, will become the Supreme Brahman, thereby attaining immortality. (60)

Bhagavan's comment: This is the secret of the Nath Panth. Here comes "I am That" or "That Am I"–Soham. Our system also says this. Meditate thus for a long time on the Self. You have to say repeatedly: "That I Am"–Soham. This sixtieth verse is very important.

Gradually they will learn to cast away their childish pranks and desire to delight like yourself. As they watch your Peace, they will themselves recoil from their vagaries.

Through diligent practice of Soham japa as outlined in *Soham Yoga: The Yoga of the Self*, all the aspects of the mind will become

unified and oriented toward the Self in which they will delight
and "cast away their childish pranks."

The first time I meditated on Soham, at one point I inwardly
said: "Oh! I love this!" And I never changed my mind. Every
meditation is a wonder and a delight.

*Continue the worship patiently. Be not led away by the vagaries
of the mind.*

The author has spoken about the "children" of the mental
modes, and now is speaking about their "parent," the mind itself
from which they spring.

The mind has two vagaries: doubt and distraction.

The doubting vagaries are: Is this really going to work? If so,
is it really the best mantra? Will this work for *me*? Can I be sure?
Will it do what its teachers say? Can I trust those who advocate
Soham sadhana? How will I know if I am doing it right? How
long will it take to produce results? What about all the other
methods that are supposed to be the best? Why don't more
people practice this one? Can something so simple as this work
and lead to enlightenment? The mind is creative, so there can
be a lot more, but just keep on mentally intoning *So* when you
inhale and *Ham* [pronounced Hum] when you exhale.

Distraction is when the mind suggests other things to do,
such as pointing out that you aren't feeling "on target" today
so you should wait until later in the day or until tomorrow to
meditate. Or that there is something you really had better do
instead of meditating "right now." There are variations on this,
the sole purpose being getting you to quit or do something

pointless like "walking meditation" or opening your eyes in meditation instead of keeping them closed, or bothering with hand mudras or strenuous and uncomfortable postures rather than just sitting upright and relaxed.

Another form of distraction is meant to get you to not simply practice as described, but to add to it or vary it, such as intoning Soham at the chakras, doing alternate nostril breathing while intoning Soham with the breath, or intoning the whole word Soham when inhaling and the whole word Soham when exhaling–anything but the simple way of mentally intoning *So* when you inhale and *Ham* when you exhale.

And another form of distraction is suggesting you do other practices you may already know, just in case they are really better than Soham sadhana. Or at least do them for some time during your meditation so you can compare them with each other–even though you may have done them before you learned about Soham and already know how they compare with Soham sadhana.

That is the nature of the unpurified and undisciplined mind. Ignore it and practice and experience Soham sadhana in peace.

On the contrary, they should become peaceful by your peace. All must get peace.

By your perseverance and refusal to be deflected from Soham sadhana, all doubts and distractions will fade away and leave you in peace. The Bhagavad Gita (2:65) says of such a yogi: "To obey the Atman is his peaceful joy; sorrow melts into that clear peace: his quiet mind is soon established in peace." This peace must be attained by all who seek for Self-realization. Otherwise: "The uncontrolled mind does not guess that the Atman is present: how can it meditate? Without meditation, where is peace? Without peace, where is happiness?" (Bhagavad Gita 2:66).

10. I shall finish in one word: The essence of all the Vedas is "Peace."

That peace is based on abhaya–fearlessness; a state of steadfastness in which one is not swayed by fear of any kind, and there is no worry or upset regarding anything. I personally, in over half a century of "yoga" practice, never experienced this until I began Soham sadhana. And then it came about in only two or three weeks, and has remained.

CHAPTER FIVE–ACTION

1. All action is God's. His power has fixed each thing into its own individual function. By His agency the insentient objects and the sentient beings do their work. All actions are His.

2. All are doing their respective work. So what has God to do with it? We will first consider the sentient beings and, later on, the insentient objects. We are sentient beings. Let us first see whose actions are ours. We all desire a higher state and work for it. But our achievements are not uniform. Sometimes the goal is the same and so is the work, but why is there a difference in the results? Here God makes us understand that the action is His. Otherwise all must be alike. The difference in the conditions cannot be accounted for. Can there be anyone who does not wish to improve his position? Whatever their intention towards others, their intention towards themselves is surely honest. The conditions of people of the same intention are yet different. This is because all actions are of God.

3. All beings have the same intention; yet their efforts are of different degrees, so also their states. After saying this, the question arises: What is effort? Is it not simply a mental image? All these images have the same origin, namely, the common intention of all. Why then should the image of effort differ in each? Here too God makes us see that all actions are His.

4. If it is said that notwithstanding the same intention, the effort can vary according to individual capacity, the question arises: What is the source of this capacity? It is of the body and mind. The environment may also affect it. One must take account of all the factors before one makes an effort. However, these factors are not under one's control so that the effort may not be equal to the task. Therefore all actions are God's.

5. Again, if it is said that the body, the mind and the environment will gradually be made equal to the task, it implies a present incapacity. This is to admit that all actions are God's.

6. Now, is it for good or bad that people do not gain their objectives? It is certainly good. Why? Most of them are selfish. Judge for yourself if their success is for the good of the world or otherwise. You may ask: Should not the attempts of the unselfish be entirely successful? Though to all appearances they may look unselfish, yet they are not free from blemishes. These depend on the ego. If the imagined unselfishness has given rise to a sense of superiority over others, God frustrates their purpose and teaches them that "You are also like others and I govern you." On the other hand, free from selfishness and free from ego is the representative of God, within whom the cloud of ego that conceals God does not exist and from whom God is ever shining forth. To such a one of true purpose (Sattva Sankalpa) all his intentions come out true. God shines forth directly in him. There is no darkness in him. Only he knows the Divine purpose as it is. Through him God fulfils the purpose of His creation. All actions are God's.

7. If it is asked: Is there not a single person of true intent? And why should not the world have all blessings in full? The

answer, which is a secret, is that the sages who are aware that all actions are God's, wish to make it known to others as well. There is no greater good than to know that all actions are God's and not our own. This knowledge contains all the blessings in itself. Therefore the intention of the sages is to clearly instruct others in the knowledge of God and His actions. Even so, they do not say "Know God this very instant," but they teach the ways and means to knowledge and encourage us in right conduct – this much only. They do not say, "Be emancipated at once." Why? Because this is not possible for the common people. Nor do the sages say to God, "Liberate the people at once." Because the sages are free from the ego and think, "God knows what He should do and when to do it. What is there for me to say to Him?" Thus they wish only to do their work, without any interest in the fruits this work may produce. They have known that God alone dispenses the fruits of actions. Simply they watch the course of events in the world and do their work, never thinking of creating a world of their own. Why? To do so is a form of egoism. The creation is as it should be. Everything is in order. All actions are God's.

8. Knowing their actions are subservient to the Higher Power, how could they hope to achieve something dear to their hearts? No, they cannot. They will do their work simply as a duty. The scriptures say, "Do work, but do not think of its fruits." Just as anger unconsciously overpowers a man even though he is determined not to get angry, so also the sages of true intent (Sattva Sankalpa) may be shocked by the iniquities of the world and unwittingly think, "God, let that be made good!" If so, then it will

certainly happen and good will prevail. This is the cause of some extraordinary events in the world. These extraordinary events are the results of a wish stealing into the mind of a sage. This is the law of nature. Who can change it? All actions are God's.

9. Whatever takes place, it is in the natural order of things. Also, it is right. Everything happens by His will alone. In truth, it is not wrong to think "He makes the thief steal." Why? Because at the time of punishment He also makes the thief suffer for the robbery. Thus, there should be no ill-will directed towards the thief. Such is the fruit of the knowledge that all actions are God's. Although there is no ill-will towards the thief, there is a dislike of theft. This is also the result of our knowledge that all actions are God's. How is this? Because the thief himself dislikes theft: Would he keep quiet if his own belongings were stolen by another? He would not. Who can be unaware that good is right and evil is wrong? Therefore the knowledge that all actions are God's will bring into the world an era of orderly conduct. Our knowledge does not extend further. We can repeat only what we know. We need not worry about what lies beyond our knowledge. This too is God's will.

10. One of the fruits of knowledge granted to us by God is the knowledge that all actions are God's. We are powerless to ask God, "Why do you act thus?" Because the fruits of our actions are not always according to our desire, all religions admit similar states of our powerlessness. In other words, because our powers are limited, we cannot but say that all actions are God's. The law which applies to us, applies to insentient objects also. Our law is no better than theirs. All is one. Even though some do

not admit that all actions are God's, yet they admit their own incapacity. This itself is the act of God.

Commentary

1. All action is God's. His power has fixed each thing into its own individual function. By His agency the insentient objects and the sentient beings do their work. All actions are His.

All action is God's.

Since God is all things and is all power–Shiva and Shakti–all action by its very nature has to be God's, and in the highest view, God itself. Nothing occurs that is not the action of God, even though God has in a sense "loaned" power to sentient beings so that through their will (another form of power) they can act, reap their actions and thereby evolve until they themselves are revealed as God. The entire range of relative existence and all that takes place within it is totally the Divine Shakti.

His power has fixed each thing into its own individual function.

All differentiation is also the act of God as is the entire range of Life. The principle is simple: everything is God–both being and action.

By His agency the insentient objects and the sentient beings do their work. All actions are His.

God is the inner life and power of all things, animate and inanimate. God is absolutely the Antaryamin: the indweller, inner guide, and inner ruler. Therefore all actions are His. But if we have an externalized, mechanistic concept of relative existence, then a multitude of questions and objections arise–all logical to our finite minds but nonetheless foolish and irrelevant. But if we realize that all things are appearance, simple concepts in the Absolute Consciousness, Parabrahman–that God is in a sense only conceptualizing or "dreaming" the entire range of relative existence, and all sentient beings are part of his dream and dreamers along with him–then we can get some glimmer of how things are with us.

"Do not say: 'God gave us this delusion.' You dream you are the doer, you dream that action is done, you dream that action bears fruit. It is your ignorance, it is the world's delusion that gives you these dreams" (Bhagavad Gita 5:14).

Everything else in this chapter–which you have already read at the beginning of this book–simply reinforces and considers aspects of the nature of action. So it needs no comment in my opinion. We need only set in mind what the author says about these aspects and see and act accordingly. This first section of the chapter says it all; the rest is elaboration to bring the truths home to us.

However, I do believe that the key to understanding this chapter is to always keep in mind that action is karma which is an inexorable law that governs all relative existence through its aspect of reaction in response to action. Again: "You dream you are the doer, you dream that action is done, you dream that action bears fruit."

Only when we understand the dream nature of relative existence which is the ladder of evolution can we understand about ourselves within it and how to make our ascent through many lives until perfect Self-realization is attained by each one of us.

CHAPTER SIX–THE EGO AND THE ATMAN

Since the author is not around to ask, and since I do not know Tamil, the original language of the text, only its English translation, I have changed the wording in this chapter in relation to the ego and the Self—including the chapter title—because it is confusing and misleading. Sometimes the ahankara (ego) is addressed and at other times the Self, the jivatman, of someone who has not realized his true Self-nature is addressed. Yet "ego" is used in all instances, and Brahman is called Universal Ego, rather than the Paramatman, the Supreme Self. (The commentator).

1. Oh ego [ahankara], false self, all the evils of the world are from you. To crush you, the kings make laws and the wise give lessons. In spite of their efforts from time immemorial, alas! you are yet alive; you simply go into hiding and reappear again and again. Can there be no end to you? Yea, it is surely approaching. Another, true Self has started to kill you. It is the knowledge, the Consciousness, of the Universal Self, the Paramatman, referred to in the Mahavakya *Aham Brahmasmi*: "I am Brahman."

2. Oh ego, think not that your enemy is of your kind. You are perishable whereas He is not. You are conceited as "I" because

you always differentiate as "I," "you" and "he," but your enemy is free from this conceit. How? He harmonizes all differences, resolves all into Himself. Moreover, you feel enmity towards Him because He has arisen to kill you. But He has no ill-feelings towards you. How is this? Because you are not to be found in His presence. He regards you as a part of His limbs. Your loss in his proximity is the working of your own falsity; He would not think of killing you because you are of no consequence in His sight. Therefore, ego, you are His enemy, but He is not yours. More briefly put, you are your own enemy. Why? Owing to your greed you flaunted yourself before the Great One as you would elsewhere. Instantly, you were lost; therefore, the Universal Self obscures you by devouring you and then shines forth as All-light.

3. Oh ego, the evils of your works have no limits. You are not content unless you are exalted above others and others are lowered before you. Endless are your desires, such as "By what title shall I gain honor?" "In what form shall I appear elegant?" "Do others bow to me? Do others obey me in silence?" "Do others say that no one excels me?" Alas! How short is your life! And yet to how much do you aspire! And how much evil you do! You have deluded yourself that there is happiness in such ideas and in differentiating yourself from all others. This is not to your good. Why not? Are not others also entitled to all these? What is your share in things which are common to millions and millions of others? Such being the case, do not desire in vain to rule over all. By your vain desire you bring about evil to yourself and to others.

Oh jivatman, individual Self, in the hypnotic grip of this terrible evil of ahankara! Listen to my friendly advice. Truly speaking, He whom you regard as your mortal enemy because you identify with the ego is your friend. He knows how to make you worthy of true greatness and blessings. Surrender to Him. This Universal Self does not treat you as an enemy but is your greatest benefactor.

4. By no means can you discover what He will make of you unless you surrender yourself to Him. However much I may speak of it, you cannot understand. It is a matter of experience. Doubtless He will do nothing less than exalt you to His state. Therefore, be not perplexed about your future; directly surrender yourself. You can always turn away if joy does not overtake you from the very instant of surrender. Just as the drinking of milk starts with an agreeable taste and ends with the satisfaction of hunger, so also surrender starts with delight and ends with Perfect Bliss, which lies beyond even pleasure and pain. Therefore your goal, without doubt, is this Universal Self (I-Am-Brahman).

5. O jivatman, true individual Self, what will be your new name after surrender? There is no name besides yours. The Vedas laud you; the world praises you; the essence of religious teachings is yourself. Then what is your form? All forms are yours. There is no form which is not yours. What is installed in the temples of worship is you; what is described in the Vedas is you; festivities and celebrations are all for you. Now what can be your power? In your presence the world is active; each is what it is, because of you. Briefly said, all things glorify you and bear witness to your being. They are duty bound to do so. You would not have

even dreamt that this will be your state. Start at once, be not self-conceited. The Universal Self, the Paramatman, awaits you.

6. Do you wish to wake up from your dream or continue in it? How long will the dream images last? Be not idle, shake off your sleep, wake up! You are witnessing your own mental images and imagining more and more. It is all in vain. Just find out who it is that sees the visions. Do not delude yourself that you are these that rise and sink in you. Wake up. The instant you wake up you will know that waking is better than this dream. Get up! The Universal Self waits to rejoice at seeing you awake.

7. Fear not the cessation of the present ego dream. Once you are awake you will enjoy the same all the more. You will no longer be deluded and will observe it with cheerful detachment, unconfused. The folly of all appearances will be understood and you will have no burdens. In dream your mental imagery assumes shapes. On waking you know the dream as just a dream. Do not mistake dream for the waking state. Know the dream as dream. For doing so, you must reach the state of "I-am-Brahman" (the Universal Self) and wake from the illusion of the ego.

8. I have instructed you for your good and not in my own interest. If you believe me, you should act upon what I have taught you. On the other hand, if you see no good in what I have said, then turn away from this ideal. How can I help you if my advice and all the advice of the saints do not make any impression on you? No state is higher than this. Believe me, it is for your good that you realize this truth; and through you others may realize the same. Be free from self-conceit. Start at once. Realize that the Universal Self is your own.

9. Oh jivatman, see how you are a slave to all and therefore suffer. How pitiable is your state! All are hostile to you! When you say "for me only," all others will also contend "for me only, for me only." When you say "I am great," they protest, "Why? We are also." All are hostile to you. Owing to the troubles caused by others, your mental images increase a millionfold. Should you not rise above them and profit by surrendering to a Master? Then all your enemies will befriend you. If you say to others, "All these are yours," everyone becomes your friend. There is only One who can make you that magnanimous and that is "I-am-Brahman" (Universal Self).

10. I shall say one word only and this is not owing to my egoism. It is simply my duty. I do not say this word just for your or my good alone. It is for the good of all.

The truth is "I-am-Brahman" (Universal Self).

Commentary

1. Oh ego [ahankara], false self, all the evils of the world are from you.

This is a very sober and correct assessment of ego and the evils it has unleashed upon the world through those in its grip. Since everything is essentially consciousness, and the human being is essentially conscious, a person's mind which is formed of intelligent energy (shakti) often seems to have a life of its own. For this reason the ego–which is part of the lower mind–is being spoken to like this.

From ego comes countless negative things such as pride, arrogance, violence, deceit, oppression and crimes of many kinds, including murder. Ego is the demon within, and those who do not realize this are susceptible to its devious ways. The yogi especially must know this, for nothing is more hateful to the ego than the prospect of its weakening or complete dissolution by the attainment of higher consciousness. The means to that attainment is yoga sadhana, the most effective of all approaches and practices, and thus the most important. Consequently the ego will do everything in its power (which is given to it by the individual) to prevent the yogi from engaging in sadhana. This is done in many ways in order to either stop the yogi from continuing his sadhana or in some way to reduce or ruin the practice–which includes getting him to practice the worthless or harmful methods of false yoga propagated by false gurus.

To crush you, the kings make laws and the wise give lessons. In spite of their efforts from time immemorial, alas! you are yet alive; you simply go into hiding and reappear again and again.

This is especially so since the ego masquerades as the yogi's true Self, the Atman. And it is most adept at hiding itself behind its machinations and even fooling the yogi into thinking that its impulses are coming from either himself or from higher beings– even from God. Also the ego hides for awhile and lulls the sadhaka into thinking that he has "conquered the ego," only to reappear even worse and stronger than before.

Can there be no end to you? Yea, it is surely approaching. Another, True Self has started to kill you. It is the knowledge, the

Consciousness, of the Universal Self, the Paramatman, referred to in the Mahavakya Aham Brahmasmi: "I am Brahman."

This is why those around the beginner yogi often become relentless foes of his yoga sadhana. Their egos are being unsettled by the change in him. But it is the yogi himself that is responsible for his turning from the upward path, often saying that he was "losing control of" his own mind and life, even often denouncing yoga as "of the devil" if he is religiously inclined. The reason this occurs is simple: yoga sadhana carried on intensely and continuously in time banishes the ego from its usurped throne and dissolves it in the dawning of the Consciousness of the Universal Self, the Paramatman whose very Presence in the yogi's consciousness is the awareness: "I Am Brahman." If the yogi identifies with the ego he feels pressured and even becomes fearful, thinking that he might die either by losing his mind or ruining his health in some way. Clinging to his false self and his false life—both of which must "die"—he turns from the path of light back into his former darkness which he is used to and finds comfortable. Or he does so, afraid and intimidated by the threatenings and dire predictions of his ego and the egos of those around him.

Speaking as the consciousness of his own revealed Self, Jesus said: "A man's foes shall be they of his own household. Whosoever therefore shall confess me before men, him will I confess also before my Father which is in heaven. But whosoever shall deny me before men, him will I also deny before my Father which is in heaven. Think not that I am come to send peace on earth: I came not to send peace, but a sword. For I am come to set a man at variance against his father, and the daughter against her mother, and the daughter in law against her mother in law. And a man's foes shall be they of his own household. He that loveth father or mother more than me is not worthy of me: and he that loveth son or daughter more than me is not worthy of me. And he that taketh not his cross, and followeth after me, is not worthy of me. He that findeth his life shall lose it: and he that loseth his life for my sake shall find it" (Matthew 10:36-39).

2. Oh ego, think not that your enemy is of your kind. You are perishable whereas He is not.

The Self and the ego are exact opposites: one is real and the other is both an illusion and a delusion. Where the ego reigns the Self remains unknown, but where the Self is revealed the ego vanishes like the mirage it actually is. Only the yogi can come to know and experience this.

You are conceited as "I" because you always differentiate as "I," "you" and "he," but your enemy is free from this conceit.

The consciousness of Unity–of the Self with the Supreme Self; of the jivatman with the Paramatman–dispels the false ego which is like a person with crossed eyes who always sees two when there is really only one.

How? He harmonizes all differences, resolves all into Himself.

This is to be known by every yogi as the "innermost secret: knowledge of God which is nearer than knowing, open vision direct and instant" (Bhagavad Gita 9:1).

Moreover, you feel enmity towards Him because he has arisen to kill you. But He has no ill-feelings towards you. How is this? Because you are not to be found in His presence. He regards you as a part of His limbs.

The Self does not perceive the ego as a reality, and so cannot have any reaction to it at all. Since the ego is an entity formed of mayic shakti, it can be considered a momentary extension of the atma shakti that the Self knows as ultimately unreal.

Your loss in His proximity is the working of your own falsity; He would not think of killing you because you are of no consequence in His sight. Therefore, ego, you are His enemy, but He is not yours.

God, being Absolute Reality, there is no possibility of his relating to what is not fundamentally real. At the active presence of the Self the ego dissolves, but it is not from any enmity on the part of God or the Self. Rather, being unreal, the Reality dispels its false appearance, for the ego exists only as a mirage, an hallucination. Therefore all that is done under the influence of ego is equally unreal to those who have attained the Self.

More briefly put, you are your own enemy. Why? Owing to your greed you flaunted yourself before the Great One as you would elsewhere. Instantly, you were lost; therefore, the Universal Self obscures you by devouring you and then shines forth as All-light.

There it is in the proverbial nutshell! May we embody this Truth through ourselves shining forth as All-light.

3. Oh ego, the evils of your works have no limits. You are not content unless you are exalted above others and others are lowered before you. Endless are your desires, such as "By what title shall I gain honor?" "In what form shall I appear elegant?" "Do others bow to me? Do others obey me in silence?" "Do others say that no one excels me?"

Alas! How short is your life! And yet to how much do you aspire! And how much evil you do!

You have deluded yourself that there is happiness in such ideas and in differentiating yourself from all others. This is not to your good. Why not? Are not others also entitled to all these? What is your share in things which are common to millions and millions of others? Such being the case, do not desire in vain to rule over all. By your vain desire you bring about evil to yourself and to others.

Oh jivatman, individual Self, in the hypnotic grip of this terrible evil of ahankara! Listen to my friendly advice. Truly speaking, He whom you regard as your mortal enemy because you identify with the ego is your friend.

It is a terrible thing to see our ego-enemy as a friend and our Atman-Self as an enemy when in reality the Self is our only friend. Therefore: "What is man's will and how shall he use it? Let him put forth its power to uncover the Atman, not hide the Atman: man's will is the only friend of the Atman: his will is also the Atman's enemy. For when a man is self-controlled, his will is the Atman's friend. But the will of an uncontrolled man is hostile to the Atman, like an enemy" (Bhagavad Gita 6:5-6).

He knows how to make you worthy of true greatness and blessings.
Take refuge [sharanam] in Him. This Universal Self does not treat
you as an enemy but is your greatest benefactor.

Often we find stated in spiritual writings that we should
"surrender" to God and the Self. But we are at war with God and
the Self only as a result of our delusion. We need not surrender
to God and the Self, for they are not our enemies. Rather, we
need to become sharanagatis and take refuge in God and the Self.
Then we will be safe from ego and its ploys and hallucinations.
As the Gita counsels us:

"Seek refuge in enlightenment" (2:49).

"Flying from fear, from lust and anger, he hides in me his
refuge, his safety: burnt clean in the blaze of my being, in me
many find home" (Bhagavad Gita 4:10).

"Therefore, having severed with the sword of your own
knowledge this doubt that proceeds from ignorance abiding in
your heart, arise! Take refuge in yoga" (4:42).

"With mind absorbed in me, practicing yoga, taking refuge
in me, hear how without doubt you shall know me completely"
(7:1).

"Truly this divine illusion (maya) of mine made of the gunas
(gunamayi) is difficult to go beyond (penetrate; master). Verily
only those who attain me (take refuge in me) shall pass beyond
this illusion (maya)" (7:14).

"At the end of many births the wise man takes refuge in me.
He knows: All is Vasudeva [He Who Dwells in All Things]. How
very rare is that great soul" (7:19).

'Those who strive toward freedom from old age and dying,

taking refuge in me, know Brahman totally, and know the Self [Adhyatma] and karma perfectly" (7:29).

"[I am] the Goal, the Sustainer, the Lord, the Witness, the Abode, the Refuge, the Friend, the Origin (Birth), the Dissolution, the Foundation, the Treasure house and the Imperishable (Eternal) Seed" (9:18).

"Truly, those who take refuge in me... attain the Supreme Goal" (9:32).

"Then that place is to be sought to which, having gone, they do not return again: 'In that Primeval Purusha from which streamed forth the ancient Power, I take refuge'" (15:4).

"Doing all actions always, taking refuge in me, by my grace he attains the eternal, immutable (imperishable) state (abode)" (18:56).

"The Lord dwells in the hearts of all beings, causing them by his maya to revolve as if mounted on a machine. Fly unto him alone for refuge with your whole being. By that grace you shall attain supreme peace and the eternal abode" (18:61-62).

"Abandoning all duties, take refuge in me alone; then I shall free (liberate) you from all evils (sins; demerits), do not grieve" (18:66).

4. By no means can you discover what He will make of you unless you take refuge in Him.

I wish I knew exactly what the Tamil original says here, because quite frankly I am not comfortable with the idea that the Absolute will "make" something of me, when in reality we can never be anything but what we already are: the Self. Certainly the

Self is to be revealed or realized, and that will necessarily bring about a change in my prakriti, in the manifest part of me that is an adjunct, but not in my eternal, permanent atman. Nothing can be added to that or taken away from it. The dream will definitely change, but the dreamer will never be changed. Otherwise Non-duality is not the prevailing truth of all existence. The Self cannot be changed, any more than Brahman, its Essence, can be changed. I grew up with this "clay in the potter's hand" view of man and God, but it is nonsense and prevents its adherents from seeing the truth about themselves. And it keeps them from seeking the truth of their own being, which they cannot find (discover) unless they actively seek it.

However much I may speak of it, you cannot understand. It is a matter of experience.

This is certainly the truth; so why are there volumes and volumes of "Advaita" philosophy that claim to reveal the reality of our essential non-dual being to us by our mere reading of their words? When the future Swami Turiyananda met Sri Ramakrishna he told him that he studied Advaita texts for several hours a day. Ramakrishna was amazed and asked him why he needed to do such a thing since Shankara himself had written: "I shall tell you in half a sloka [verse] what has been written in tens of millions of books: Brahman is real. The world is illusory. The jiva is nothing other than Brahman." This is why the Gita speaks of the "innermost secret: knowledge of God which is nearer than knowing, open vision direct and instant" (9:1), which can only be attained through yoga sadhana. We must KNOW the Self.

Doubtless He will do nothing less than exalt you to His state. Therefore, be not perplexed about your future; directly take refuge in Him.

Here again I could use an accurate translation. It is true that in the matter of Self-realization Seeing Is Becoming. But only for the yogi. Not for anyone else. And since we engage in the sadhana that gives us the transforming experience, it is not amiss to say that we exalt/enlighten ourselves. For our Self is what we seek—not the Self of another. And we awaken to the fact of the Self's reality through our intellect that is illumined by our intuition—not through the intellect of anyone else. And we realize the Self throughout own effort, through our own sadhana practice—not through the action of anyone else. Not even through God, though it is only through the divine power that we are able to realize the Self.

In *Light of Soham* there is the following exchange between Mr. Moreshwarrao Mathure and Sri Gajanana Maharaj.

Mathure: It is said that one must have the support (adhishthana) of God. Please explain to me what is meant by this.

Maharaj: Mathure, you have learnt too much Vedanta. I myself feel that there is no support of any thing to any other thing. Do not pay any attention to the above-mentioned saying regarding the support of God. Try to get the support of your own Self. Make the three things one: the meditator, the act of meditation and the entity to be meditated upon. And be absorbed into the state of joy. It will be of no use reading and discussing about what is written in thousands of books. In order to attain one's goal three things are necessary: association with saints, devotion towards one's guru and disgust with worldly life. If your conduct is pure, if you try to follow the principles of morality, and your mind is full of disinterested devotion and you repeat the mantra given by your guru, your mind is sure to be ultimately purified. He who experiences the joy of his own Self naturally and easily follows these rules of conduct!

You can always turn away if joy does not overtake you from the very instant of taking refuge.

Just as the drinking of milk starts with an agreeable taste and ends with the satisfaction of hunger, so also taking refuge starts with delight and ends with Perfect Bliss, which lies beyond even pleasure and pain. Therefore your goal, without doubt, is this Universal Self (I-Am-Brahman).

Great relief and happiness and ease of heart–parama sukha–arises in those who truly take refuge in the Self by devoting themselves to yoga sadhana and the complete observance of Sanatana Dharma in all its aspects and principles. Yogananda, Dharmananda, Satyananda and Purnananda shall be theirs always.

5. O jivatman, true individual Self, what will be your new name after taking refuge? There is no name besides yours.

And that name is Paramatmananda: the Bliss of the Supreme Self.

The Vedas laud you; the world praises you; the essence of religious teachings is yourself.

For you are Purnaparamatmananda: The Full Joy Of The Supreme Self.

Then what is your form? All forms are yours. There is no form which is not yours.

What is installed in the temples of worship is you; what is described in the Vedas is you; festivities and celebrations are all for you.

Now what can be your power? In your presence the world is active; each is what it is, because of you.

Briefly said, all things glorify you and bear witness to your being. They are duty bound to do so.

You would not have even dreamt that this will be your state.

Start at once, be not self-conceited.

The Universal Self, the Paramatman, awaits you.

It only remains for you to awaken in yourself the Reality that has always been there. And how shall it be awakened? "Be a yogi" (Bhagavad Gita 6:46).

6. Do you wish to wake up from your dream or continue in it? How long will the dream images last? Be not idle, shake off your sleep, wake up!

The call to us is that with which Swami Vivekananda, continually exhorted his hearers: "Awake! Arise! And stop not until you reach the Goal!"

How? "Be a yogi."

You are witnessing your own mental images and imagining more and more. It is all in vain. Just find out who it is that sees the visions.

That "Who" is the true "I" in the Mahavakya *Aham Brahmasmi*: your own Self. *Tat Twam Asi*: That You Are!

Do not delude yourself that you are these images and imaginings that rise and sink in you.

At the beginning of this commentary I mentioned that when Sri Ramakrishna was asked, "What is the Self?" he replied: "The witness of the mind." Now the author is reminding us that all of our sensory experiences, our thoughts and feelings–all that is based on our external awareness–are "images and imaginings" that are only neurological interpretations of the outside things which stimulate our senses which in turn relay the impulses to the brain which are interpreted by the mind. To identify with these impressions and say, "This is me" in response to them is a grave mistake. For we are never the witnessed–only the witness. The only satisfactory answer to the question "who are you?" is "consciousness itself." Consciousness is both the who and the what of our existence. Again we come back to the truth that all is a dream, the only reality being the dreamer.

The impressions that rise and subside solely in our mind can never be our true Self. But nearly all beings in relative existence are drowned in the illusion that they are.

Wake up. The instant you wake up you will know that waking is better than this dream. Get up! The Universal Self waits to rejoice at seeing you awake.

This is good advice, but how do we awake? There is only one process of awakening into reality: yoga sadhana. So in a sense the only real thing we ever do is sadhana.

7. Fear not the cessation of the present ego dream. Once you are awake you will enjoy the same all the more. You will no longer be deluded and will observe it with cheerful detachment, unconfused. The folly of all appearances will be understood and you will have no burdens.

There can be fear of awakening and ending the dream, but that fear is the fear of the ego, the fear of the ego-mirage that knows it will cease to exist upon our awakening. Those that identify with the ego will both hate and fear the truth of our Self and the possibility that we can awaken into it and leave egoic delusions behind forever. But our true Self will rejoice in the freedom it will gain after creation cycles of being deluded and bound.

There is a joke about a drunk man who was walking along with one foot on the sidewalk and the other down on the street. Someone stopped him and asked, "What are you doing walking with one foot on the walk and the other in the street?" "I am?" spluttered the man, who looked down and burst into tears and exclaimed, "Thank God! I thought I was a cripple!" That is how it will be with us when we awaken from the ego-dream.

In dream your mental imagery assumes shapes. On waking you know the dream as just a dream. Do not mistake dream for the waking state. Know the dream as dream. For doing so, you must reach the state of "I-am-Brahman" (the Universal Self) and wake from the illusion of the ego.

And that is done very simply by awakening into the consciousness of Soham: I Am That. And Soham Sadhana, Soham Yoga, is the way to awaken.

8. I have instructed you for your good and not in my own interest.

It is a rare thing to find a "spiritual teacher" who is teaching for the good of others rather than his own reputation, benefit and gain of disciples. But such do exist, and when found should be valued highly and listened to and taken seriously. For a picture of a true and worthy teacher, read *Light of Soham*, for Sri Gajanana Maharaj was an ideal example of both student and teacher.

If you believe me, you should act upon what I have taught you.

It may seem strange that someone might believe something and yet not act upon that belief. But billions are doing so this day, and will continue to do so for the rest of their lives. We, however, should be wise and true to ourselves and act without delay, realizing that in all things there are tides which help and tides which hinder. The moment we learn of higher truths that is itself evidence that if we act upon them we will succeed in spiritual attainment. But any delay may bring about a shift in the karmic tides that govern all of us, and we may miss the opportunity to realize those truths.

On the other hand, if you see no good in what I have said, then turn away from this ideal.

This is exactly what a worthy–and therefore an honest and responsible–teacher will say to you. Consider what he says and either act or do not act upon his words. At all times you must be in complete charge of your spiritual life. The decision to follow the counsel of a teacher should be in your hands alone. Any teacher who tries to cajole or push you into anything in any manner is a fraud and a danger to you. Avoid such a one, and flee if you are already in his influence. Only harm can come to you from such a person.

How can I help you if my advice and all the advice of the saints do not make any impression on you?

The mind is a field of magnetic energy. According to its polarity it perceives and is attracted to something that is on its own vibratory level or character. Unless someone is on the same "frequency" of an idea or a teacher, no lasting impression or effect can occur. If we wish to attune ourselves to the right wave length, the vibration of truth, we must immerse ourselves in sadhana that will open our understanding and awareness to spiritual realities. There is no other way, for sadhana alone develops the spiritual consciousness.

No state is higher than this. Believe me, it is for your good that you realize this truth; and through you others may realize the same.

This is absolutely so.

Be free from self-conceit.

Ego is the great obstacle to all genuine spiritual unfoldment.

Start at once.

There is no tomorrow or Later On. There is only Now. Those who cultivate the habit of delay have already defeated themselves.

Realize that the Universal Self is your own.

Aspire to this Supreme Ideal alone. Then set about to realize it through Soham Sadhana and come to know without any doubt: Soham–I Am That.

9. Oh jivatman, see how you are a slave to all and therefore suffer. How pitiable is your state! All are hostile to you! When you say "for me only," all others will also contend "for me only, for me only." When you say "I am great," they protest, "Why? We are also." All are hostile to you. Owing to the troubles caused by others, your mental images increase a millionfold. Should you not rise above them and profit by taking refuge in a Master?

These words demonstrate that you and you alone are the master of your fate. What you choose is what you will have. Let there be no more delay.

Then all your enemies will befriend you. If you say to others, "All these are yours," everyone becomes your friend. There is only One who can make you that magnanimous and that is "I-am-Brahman" (the Universal Self).

When the turnaround is complete and permanent, then the universe itself becomes the sadhaka's best friend in finding and treading the way. The doors will open and the path shine before you. You will find it to be so. As Buddha said: "Turn around and lo! The other shore."

10. I shall say one word only and this is not owing to my egoism. It is simply my duty. I do not say this word just for your or my good alone. It is for the good of all.

The truth is "I-am-Brahman" (Universal Self).
Nothing more need be said.
Farewell.

Did you enjoy reading this book?

Thank you for taking the time to read *All Is One*. If you enjoyed it, please consider telling your friends or posting a short review at Amazon.com, Goodreads, or the site of your choice.

Word of mouth is an author's best friend and much appreciated

GET YOUR FREE MEDITATION GUIDE

Sign up for the Light of the Spirit Newsletter and get *Learn How to Meditate Effectively.*

Get free updates: newsletters, blog posts, and podcasts, plus exclusive content from Light of the Spirit Monastery.

Visit: https://ocoy.org/newsletter-registration

GLOSSARY

Abhaya(m): "Without fear;" fearlessness; a state of steadfastness in which one is not swayed by fear of any kind.

Adhishthana(m): Seat; basis; substratum; ground; support; abode; the body as the abode of the subtle bodies and the Self; underlying truth or essence; background.

Adhyatma: The individual Self; the supreme Self; spirit.

Advaita: Non-dualism; non-duality; literally: not [a] two [dvaita].

Advaitic: Non-dual; having to do with the philosophy of Advaita (Non-Dualism).

Ahankara: Ego; egoism or self-conceit; the self-arrogating principle "I," "I" am-ness; self-consciousness.

Ananda: Bliss; happiness; joy. A fundamental attribute of Brahman, which is Satchidananda: Existence, Consciousness, Bliss.

Anandamayi Ma: One of the major spiritual figures in twentieth-century India, first made known to the West by Paramhansa Yogananda in his *Autobiography of a Yogi*.

Atma(n): The individual spirit or Self that is one with Brahman; the essential being, nature or identity of each sentient being.

Atmajnana: Direct knowledge of the Self; Brahma-Jnana.

Atmashakti: Power of the Self; personal power or strength.

Bhagavad Gita: "The Song of God." The sacred philosophical text often called "the Hindu Bible," part of the epic Mahabharata by Vyasa; the most popular sacred text in Hinduism.

Bhagavan: The Lord; the One endowed with the six attributes, viz. infinite treasures, strength, glory, splendor knowledge, and renunciation; the Personal God.

Bhakti: Devotion; dedication; love (of God).

Bhava: Subjective state of being (existence); attitude of mind; mental attitude or feeling; state of realization in the heart or mind.

Brahmajnana: Direct, transcendental knowledge of Brahman; Self-realization.

Brahman: The Absolute Reality; the Truth proclaimed in the Upanishads; the Supreme Reality that is one and indivisible, infinite, and eternal; all-pervading, changeless Existence; Existence-knowledge-bliss Absolute (Satchidananda); Absolute Consciousness; it is not only all-powerful but all-power itself; not only all-knowing and blissful but all-knowledge and all-bliss itself.

Buddhi: Intellect; intelligence; understanding; reason; the thinking mind; the higher mind, which is the seat of wisdom; the discriminating faculty.

Chakra: Wheel. Plexus; center of psychic energy in the human system, particularly in the spine or head.

Chit: Consciousness (that is spirit or purusha); "to perceive, observe, think, be aware, know;" pure unitary Consciousness. The principle of universal intelligence or consciousness.

Dharma: The righteous way of living, as enjoined by the sacred scriptures and the spiritually illumined; law; lawfulness; virtue; righteousness; norm.

Diksha: Initiation.

Ekam-evam-advitiyam: "One, only, without a second." A description of Brahman.

Gajanana Maharaj: Sri Gajanana Maharaj (Gajanana Murlidhar Gupte) of Nashik in western India (Maharashtra state) was a saint of the Nath Sampradaya in the first half of the twentieth century.

Guna: Quality, attribute, or characteristic arising from nature (Prakriti) itself; a mode of energy behavior. As a rule, when "guna" is used it is in reference to the three qualities of Prakriti, the three modes of energy behavior that are the basic qualities of nature, and which determine the inherent characteristics of all created things. They are: 1) sattwa–purity, light, harmony; 2) rajas–activity, passion; and 3) tamas–dullness, inertia, and ignorance.

Guru: Teacher; preceptor; spiritual teacher or acharya.

Guru Dakshina: Gift given to the guru at the time of initiation.

Ishwara: "God" or "Lord" in the sense of the Supreme Power, Ruler, Master or Controller of the cosmos. "Ishwara" implies the powers of omnipotence, omnipresence and omniscience.

Japa: Repetition of a mantra.

Jiva: Individual spirit.

Jivatma(n): Individual spirit; individual consciousness.

Jnana(m): Knowledge; knowledge of Reality–of Brahman, the Absolute; also denotes the process of reasoning by which the Ultimate Truth is attained. The word is generally used to denote the knowledge by which one is aware of one's identity with Brahman.

Jnani: A follower of the path of knowledge (jnana); one who has realized–who knows–the Truth (Brahman).

Karma: Karma, derived from the Sanskrit root *kri*, which means to act, do, or make, means any kind of action, including thought and feeling. It also means the effects of action. Karma is both action and reaction, the metaphysical equivalent of the principle: "For every action there is an equal and opposite reaction." "Whatsoever a man soweth, that shall he also reap" (Galatians 6:7). It is karma operating through the law of cause and effect that binds the jiva or the individual soul to the wheel of birth and death. There are three forms of karma: sanchita, agami, and prarabdha. Sanchita karma is the vast store of accumulated actions done in the past, the fruits of which have not yet been reaped. Agami karma is the action that will be done by the individual in the future. Prarabdha karma is the action that has begun to fructify, the fruit of which is being reaped in this life.

Karmic: Having to do with karma.

Lahiri Mahasaya: Shyama Charan Lahiri, one of the greatest yogis of nineteenth-century India, written about extensively in *Autobiography of a Yogi* by Paramhansa Yogananda.

Maharaj(a): "Great king;" lord; master; a title of respect used to address holy men.

Mahavakya: Literally: "Great Saying." The highest Vedantic truth, found in the Upanishads expressing the highest Vedantic truths or the identity between the individual soul and the Supreme Soul. There are four Mahavakyas: 1) Prajñanam Brahma–"Consciousness is Brahman" (Aitareya Upanishad 3.3); 2) Ayam Atma Brahma–"This Self is Brahman" (Mandukya Upanishad 1.2); 3) Tat Twam Asi–"Thou art That" (Chandogya Upanishad 6.8.7); 4)

Aham Brahmasmi–"I am Brahman" (Brihadaranyaka Upanishad 1.4.10).

Mantra(m): Sacred syllable or word or set of words through the repetition and reflection of which one attains perfection or realization of the Self. Literally, "a transforming thought" (manat trayate). A mantra, then is a sound formula that transforms the consciousness.

Maya: The illusive power of Brahman; the veiling and the projecting power of the universe, the power of Cosmic Illusion. "The Measurer"–a reference to the two delusive "measures," Time and Space.

Mayic: Having to do with Maya.

Meru: The mountain, of supreme height, on which the gods dwell, or the mountain on which Shiva is ever seated in meditation, said to be the center of the world, supporting heaven itself–obviously a yogic symbol of the spinal column or merudanda. The name of the central bead on a japa mala (rosary).

Moksha: Release; liberation; the term is particularly applied to the liberation from the bondage of karma and the wheel of birth and death; Absolute Experience.

Nada: Sound; the resonance of sound; mystic inner sound; the primal sound or first vibration from which all creation has emanated; the first manifestation of the unmanifested Absolute; Omkara or Shabda Brahman; the inner sound of a mantra experienced in meditation.

Nath Pantha (Nathas): Various associations of yogis who trace their roots back to Matsyendranath and the Nath Yogi Sampradaya.

Nath Yogi: A member of the Nath Yogi Sampradaya.

Nath Yogi Sampradaya: An ancient order of yogis claiming Matsyendranath, Gorakhnath, Patanjali, Jnaneshwar and Jesus (Isha Nath) among their master teachers.

Paramatma(n): The Supreme Self, God.

Prana: Life; vital energy; life-breath; life-force; inhalation. In the human body the prana is divided into five forms: 1) Prana, the prana that moves upward; 2) Apana: The prana that moves downward, producing the excretory functions in general. 3) Vyana: The prana that holds prana and apana together and produces circulation in the body. 4) Samana: The prana that carries the grosser material of food to the apana and brings the subtler material to each limb; the general force of digestion. 5) Udana: The prana which brings up or carries down what has been drunk or eaten; the general force of assimilation.

Puja: Worship; ceremonial (ritual) worship; adoration; honor. Usually involving the image of a deity.

Purna: Full; complete; infinite; absolute; Brahman.

Purusha: "Person" in the sense of a conscious spirit. Both God and the individual spirits are purushas, but God is the Adi (Original, Archetypal) Purusha, Parama (Highest) Purusha, and the Purushottama (Highest or Best of the Purushas).

Ramakrishna, Sri: Sri Ramakrishna lived in India in the second half of the nineteenth century, and is regarded by all India as a perfectly enlightened person–and by many as an Incarnation of God.

Ramana Maharshi: A great twentieth-century sage from Tamil Nadu, who lived most of his life at or on the sacred mountain of Arunachala in the town of Tiruvannamalai.

Sadhaka: One who practices spiritual discipline–sadhana–particularly meditation.

Sadhana: Spiritual practice.

Samsara: Life through repeated births and deaths; the wheel of birth and death; the process of earthly life.

Samskara: Impression in the mind, either conscious or subconscious, produced by action or experience in this or previous lives; propensities of the mental residue of impressions; subliminal activators; prenatal tendency. See Vasana.

Sanatana Dharma: "The Eternal Religion," also known as "Arya Dharma," "the religion of those who strive upward [Aryas]." Hinduism.

Sanskrit: The language of the ancient sages of India and therefore of the Indian scriptures and yoga treatises.

Satchidananda: Existence-Knowledge-Bliss Absolute; Brahman.

Shabda: Sound; word.

Shabda Brahman: Sound-God; Brahman in the Form of Sound; Soham; the Vedas.

Shakti: Power; energy; force; the Divine Power of becoming; the apparent dynamic aspect of Eternal Being; the Absolute Power or Cosmic Energy; the Divine Feminine.

Shankara: Shankaracharya; Adi (the first) Shankaracharya: The great reformer and re-establisher of Vedic Religion in India around 500 B.C. He is the unparalleled exponent of Advaita (Non-Dual) Vedanta. He also reformed the mode of monastic life and founded (or regenerated) the ancient Swami Order.

Sharanagati: One who has taken refuge or shelter, or sought protection.

Sharanam: Refuge; protection, shelter.

Shiva: A name of God meaning "One Who is all Bliss and the giver of happiness to all." Although classically applied to the Absolute Brahman, Shiva can also refer to God (Ishwara) in His aspect of Dissolver and Liberator (often mistakenly thought of as "destroyer").

Shyama Charan Lahiri: See Lahiri Mahasaya.

Siddha: A perfected–liberated–being, an adept, a seer, a perfect yogi.

Sivananda (Swami): A great twentieth-century Master, founder of the world-wide Divine Life Society, whose books on spiritual life and religion are widely circulated in the West as well as in India.

Smriti: Memory; recollection; "that which is remembered;" code of law. In this latter sense, Smriti is used to designate all scriptures except the Vedas and Upanishads (which are considered of greater authority: Shruti).

Soham: "That am I;" the ultimate Atma mantra, the mantra of the Self; the Ajapa Gayatri formula of meditation in which "So" is intoned mentally during natural inhalation and "Ham" is intoned mentally during natural exhalation. Soham is pronounced "Sohum," as the short "a" in Sanskrit is pronounced like the American "u" in "up."

Soham Bhava: The state of being and awareness: "THAT I am." Gorakhnath says that So'ham Bhava includes total Self-comprehension (ahamta), total Self-mastery (akhanda aishwarya), unbroken awareness of the unity of the Self (swatmata), awareness of the unity of the Self with all phenomenal existence–as the Self (vishwanubhava), knowledge of all within and without the Self–united in the Self (sarvajñatwa).

Sukha(m): Happiness; ease; joy; happy; pleasure; pleasant; agreeable.

Swami: Literally, "I am mine"–in the sense of absolute self-mastership. It could be legitimately translated: "He who is one with his Self [Swa]." It is often used in the sense of "lord" or owner as well as a spiritual guide or authority. God Himself is the ultimate Swami. As a matter of respect it is always used in reference to sannyasis, since they have vowed themselves to pursue the knowledge of the Self, or those considered to be of spiritual advancement.

Tapasya: Austerity; practical (i.e., result-producing) spiritual discipline; spiritual force. Literally it means the generation of heat or energy, but is always used in a symbolic manner, referring to spiritual practice and its effect, especially the roasting of karmic seeds, the burning up of karma.

Turiya: The state of pure consciousness. *A Ramakrishna-Vedanta Wordbook* defines it as: "The superconscious; lit., 'the Fourth,' in relation to the three ordinary states of consciousness–waking, dreaming, and dreamless sleep–which it transcends."

Turiya-Turiya: "The consciousness of Consciousness;" the Absolute Consciousness of God, the Consciousness behind our individualized consciousness (turiya).

Upanishads: Books (of varying lengths) of the philosophical teachings of the ancient sages of India on the knowledge of Absolute Reality. The upanishads contain two major themes: (1) the individual self (atman) and the Supreme Self (Paramatman) are one in essence, and (2) the goal of life is the realization/manifestation of this unity, the realization of God (Brahman). There are eleven principal upanishads: Isha, Kena, Katha, Prashna, Mundaka, Mandukya, Taittiriya, Aitareya, Chandogya, Brihadaranyaka, and

Shvetashvatara, all of which were commented on by Shankara, Ramanuja and Madhavacharya, thus setting the seal of authenticity on them.

Upasana: "Sitting near" or "drawing near;" worship; adoration; contemplation of God or deity; devout meditation; both teaching and learning.

Vairagya: Non-attachment; detachment; dispassion; absence of desire; disinterest; or indifference. Indifference towards and disgust for all worldly things and enjoyments.

Vasudeva: "He who dwells in all things"—the Universal God; the father of Krishna, who is himself also sometimes called Vasudeva.

Vedanta: Literally, "the end of the Vedas;" the Upanishads; the school of Hindu thought, based primarily on the Upanishads, upholding the doctrine of either pure non-dualism or conditional non-dualism. The original text of this school is Vedanta-darshana, the Brahma Sutras compiled by the sage Vyasa.

Vedas: The oldest scriptures of India, considered the oldest scriptures of the world, that were revealed in meditation to the Vedic Rishis (seers). Although in modern times there are said to be four Vedas (Rig, Sama, Yajur, and Atharva), in the upanishads only three are listed (Rig, Sama, and Yajur). In actuality, there is only one Veda: the Rig Veda. The Sama Veda is only a collection of Rig Veda hymns that are marked (pointed) for singing. The Yajur Veda is a small book giving directions on just one form of Vedic sacrifice. The Atharva Veda is only a collection of theurgical mantras to be recited for the cure of various afflictions or to be recited over the herbs to be taken as medicine for those afflictions.

Vedic: Having to do with the Vedas.

Viveka: Discrimination between the Real and the unreal, between the Self and the non-Self, between the permanent and the impermanent; right intuitive discrimination.

Vivekananda (Swami): The chief disciple of Sri Ramakrishna, who brought the message of Vedanta to the West at the end of the nineteenth century.

Yoga: Literally, "joining" or "union" from the Sanskrit root yuj. Union with the Supreme Being, or any practice that makes for such union. Meditation that unites the individual spirit with God, the Supreme Spirit. The name of the philosophy expounded by the sage Patanjali, teaching the process of union of the individual with the Universal Soul.

Yoga Nidra/Yoganidra: A state of half-contemplation and half-sleep; light yogic sleep when the individual retains slight awareness; state between sleep and wakefulness.

Yogananda (Paramhansa): The most influential yogi of the twentieth century in the West, author of *Autobiography of a Yogi* and founder of Self-Realization Fellowship in America.

Yogi: One who practices Yoga; one who strives earnestly for union with God; an aspirant going through any course of spiritual discipline.

Yogic: Having to do with Yoga.

ABOUT THE AUTHOR

A bbot George Burke (Swami Nirmala-nanda Giri) is the founder and director of the Light of the Spirit Monastery (Atma Jyoti Ashram) in Cedar Crest, New Mexico, USA.

In his many pilgrimages to India, he had the opportunity of meeting some of India's greatest spiritual figures, including Swami Sivananda of Rishikesh and Anandamayi Ma. During his first trip to India he was made a member of the ancient Swami Order by Swami Vidyananda Giri, a direct disciple of Paramhansa Yogananda, who had himself been given sannyas by the Shankaracharya of Puri, Jagadguru Bharati Krishna Tirtha.

In the United States he also encountered various Christian saints, including Saint John Maximovich of San Francisco and Saint Philaret Voznesensky of New York. He was ordained in the Liberal Catholic Church (International) to the priesthood on January 25, 1974, and consecrated a bishop on August 23, 1975.

For many years Abbot George has researched the identity of Jesus Christ and his teachings with India and Sanatana Dharma, including Yoga. It is his conclusion that Jesus lived in India for most of his life, and was a yogi and Sanatana Dharma missionary to the West. After his resurrection he returned to India and lived the rest of his life in the Himalayas.

He has written extensively on these and other topics, many of which are posted at OCOY.org.

LIGHT OF THE SPIRIT MONASTERY

Light of the Spirit Monastery is an esoteric Christian monastic community for those men who seek direct experience of the Spirit through meditation, sacramental worship, discipline and dedicated communal life, emphasizing the inner reality of "Christ in you the hope of glory," as taught by the illumined mystics of East and West.

The public outreach of the monastery is through its website, OCOY.org (Original Christianity and Original Yoga). There you will find many articles on Original Christianity and Original Yoga, including *Esoteric Christian Beliefs. Foundations of Yoga* and *How to Be a Yogi* are practical guides for anyone seriously interested in living the Yoga Life.

You will also discover many other articles on leading an effective spiritual life, including *The Yoga of the Sacraments* and *Spiritual Benefits of a Vegetarian Diet*, as well as the "Dharma for Awakening" series—in-depth commentaries on these spiritual classics: the Upanishads, the Bhagavad Gita, the Dhammapada, and the Tao Teh King.

You can listen to podcasts by Abbot George on meditation, the Yoga Life, and remarkable spiritual people he has met in India and elsewhere, at http://ocoy.org/podcasts/

READING FOR AWAKENING

Light of the Spirit Press presents books on spiritual wisdom and Original Christianity and Original Yoga. From our "Dharma for Awakening" series (practical commentaries on the world's scriptures) to books on how to meditate and live a successful spiritual life, you will find books that are informative, helpful, and even entertaining.

Light of the Spirit Press is the publishing house of Light of the Spirit Monastery (Atma Jyoti Ashram) in Cedar Crest, New Mexico, USA. Our books feature the writings of the founder and director of the monastery, Abbot George Burke (Swami Nirmalananda Giri) which are also found on the monastery's website, OCOY.org.

We invite you to explore our publications in the following pages.

Find out more about our publications at lightofthespiritpress.com

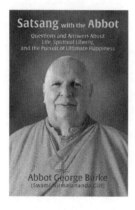

Abbot George Burke
(Swami Nirmalananda Giri)

Satsang with the Abbot

Questions & Answers about Life, Spiritual Liberty, and the Pursuit of Ultimate Happiness

Grounded in the perspective of classic Indian thought, directly taught by such luminaries as Swami Sivananda of Rishikesh and Sri Anandamayi Ma, and blessed with the clarity and originality of thought that can only come from years of spiritual practice (sadhana), Abbot George Burke's answers to inquirers' questions are unique, fresh, and authoritative.

The questions in this book range from the most sublime to the most practical. "How can I attain samadhi? " "I am married with children. How can I lead a spiritual life? " "What is Self-realization? "

In Abbot George's replies to these questions the reader will discover common sense, helpful information, and a guiding light for their journey through and beyond the forest of cliches, contradictions, and confusion of yoga, Hinduism, Christianity, and metaphysical thought.

What Readers say:

"Abbot George speaks as one who knows his subject well, and answers in an manner that conveys an effortlessness and humor that puts one at ease, while, at the same time, a wisdom and sincerity which demands an attentive ear. "—*Russ Thomas*

The Christ of India

The Story of Original Christianity

"Original Christianity" is the teaching of both Jesus of Nazareth and his Apostle Saint Thomas in India. Although it was new to the Mediterranean world, it was really the classical, traditional teachings of the ancient rishis of India that even today comprise Sanatana Dharma, the Eternal Dharma, that goes far beyond religion into realization.

In The Christ of India Abbot George Burke presents what those ancient teachings are, as well as the growing evidence that Jesus spent much of his "Lost Years" in India and Tibet. This is also the story of how the original teachings of Jesus and Saint Thomas thrived in India for centuries before the coming of the European colonialists.

What Readers say:

"Interpreting the teachings of Jesus from the perspective of Santana Dharma, The Christ of India is a knowledgeable yet engaging collection of authentic details and evident manuscripts about the Essene roots of Jesus and his 'Lost years'. ...delightful to read and a work of substance, vividly written and rich in historical analysis, this is an excellent work written by a masterful teacher and a storyteller." –*Enas Reviews*

Soham Yoga
The Yoga of the Self

An in-depth guide to the practice of Soham sadhana.

Soham (which is pronounced like "Sohum") means: I Am That. It is the natural vibration of the Self, which occurs spontaneously with each incoming and outgoing breath. By becoming aware of it on the conscious level by mentally repeating it in time with the breath (*So* when inhaling and *Ham* when exhaling), a yogi experiences the identity between his individual Self and the Supreme Self.

The practice is very simple, and the results very profound. Truly wondrous is the fact that Soham Yoga can go on all the time, not just during meditation, if we apply ourselves to it. The whole life can become a continuous stream of liberating sadhana. "By the mantra 'Soham' separate the jivatma from the Paramatma and locate the jivatma in the heart" (Devi Bhagavatam 11.8.15). When we repeat Soham in time with the breath we are invoking our eternal being. This is why we need only listen to our inner mental intonations of Soham in time with the breath which itself is Soham.

What Readers say:
"This Soham meditation has been the most simple, effective kind of meditation I have practiced... This book is a complete spiritual path" –Arnold Van Wie.

The Unknown Lives of Jesus and Mary
Compiled from Ancient Records and Mystical Revelations

"There are also many other things which Jesus did, the which, if they should be written every one, I suppose that even the world itself could not contain the books that should be written." (Gospel of Saint John, final verse)

You can discover much of those "many other things which Jesus did" in this unique compilation of ancient records and mystical revelations, which includes historical records of the lives of Jesus Christ and his Mother Mary that have been accepted and used by the Church since apostolic times. This treasury of little-known stories of Jesus' infancy, his sojourn in the Orient as recorded in the famous Ladakh Manuscript, and his passion, crucifixion, and resurrection, will broaden the reader's understanding of what Christianity really was originally.

What Readers say:
"A tough one to put down once you start reading, insightful commentaries by the author add even more rich meaning."—*Dr. William Cunningham*

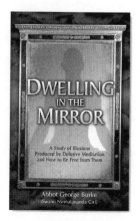

Dwelling in the Mirror
A Study of Illusions Produced by Delusive Meditation and How to Be Free from Them

"There are those who can have an experience and realize that it really cannot be real, but a vagary of their mind. Some may not understand that on their own, but can be shown by others the truth about it. For them and those that may one day be in danger of meditation-produced delusions I have written this brief study." –Abbot George Burke

In *Dwelling in the Mirror* you will learn:
- different types of meditation and the experiences they produce, and the problems and delusions which can arise from them.
- how to get rid of negative initiation energies and mantras.
- what are authentic, positive meditation practices and their effects and aspects.
- an ancient, universal method of meditation which is both proven and effective.

What Readers say:

"I totally loved this book! After running across many spiritual and self-help books filled with unrealistic promises, this little jewel had the impact of a triple Espresso."—Sandra Carrington-Smith, author of *Housekeeping for the Soul*

The Dhammapada for Awakening
A Commentary on Buddha's Practical Wisdom

The Dhammapada for Awakening brings a refreshing and timely perspective to ancient wisdom and shows seekers of inner peace practical ways to improve their inner lives today.

It explores the Buddha's answers to the urgent questions, such as "How can I find find lasting peace, happiness and fulfillment that seems so elusive?" and "What can I do to avoid many of the miseries big and small that afflict all of us?".

Drawing on the proven wisdom of different ancient traditions, and the contemporary masters of spiritual life, as well as his own studies and first-hand knowledge of the mystical traditions of East and West, Abbot George illumines the practical wisdom of Buddha in the Dhammapada, and more importantly, and make that makes that teaching relevant to present day spiritual seekers.

What Readers say:

"In this compelling book, Abbot George Burke brings his considerable knowledge and background in Christian teachings and the Vedic tradition of India to convey a practical understanding of the teachings of the Buddha. ...This is a book you'll want to take your time to read and keep as reference to reread. Highly recommended for earnest spiritual aspirants" –*Anna Hourihan, author, editor, and publisher at Vedanta Shores Press*

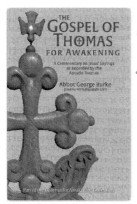

The Gospel of Thomas for Awakening
A Commentary on Jesus' Sayings as Recorded by the Apostle Thomas

"From the very beginning there were two Christianities." So begins this remarkable work. While the rest of the Apostles dispersed to various areas of the Mediterranean world, the apostle Thomas travelled to India, where growing evidence shows that Jesus spent his "Lost Years," and which had been the source of the wisdom which he had brought to the "West."

In *The Gospel of Thomas for Awakening*, Abbot George shines the "Light of the East" on the sometimes enigmatic sayings of Jesus recorded by his apostle Saint Thomas, revealing their unique and rich practical nature for modern day seekers for spiritual life. Ideal for daily study or group discussion.

What Readers say:

"An extraordinary work of theological commentary, *The Gospel of Thomas for Awakening* is as informed and informative as it is inspired and inspiring".—*James A. Cox, Editor-in-Chief, Midwest Book Review*

The Tao Teh King for Awakening
A Practical Commentary on Lao Tzu's Classic Exposition of Taoism

With penetrating insight, Abbot George Burke illumines the the wisdom of Lao Tzu's classic writing, the Tao Teh King (Tao Te Ching), and the timeless practical value of China's most beloved Taoist scripture for spiritual seekers. With a unique perspective of a lifetime of study and practice of both Eastern and Western spirituality, Abbot George mines the treasures of the Tao Teh King and presents them in an easily intelligible fashion for those wishing to put these priceless teachings into practice.

Illumined with quotes from the Gospels, the Bhagavad Gita, Yogananda and other Indian saints and Indian scriptures.

What Readers say:

"Burke's evident expertise concerning both Western and Eastern spirituality, provides readers with a wide-ranging and intriguing study of the topic. For those who seek spiritual guidance and insight into Lao Tzu's wisdom, this work offers a clear pathway." – *Publisher's Weekly (BookLife Prize)*

The Bhagavad Gita for Awakening

A Practical Commentary for Leading a Successful Spiritual Life

With penetrating insight, Abbot George Burke illumines the Bhagavad Gita's practical value for spiritual seekers. With a unique perspective from a lifetime of study and practice of both Eastern and Western spirituality, Abbot George presents the treasures of the Gita in an easily intelligible fashion.

Drawing from the teachings of Sri Ramakrishna, Jesus, Paramhansa Yogananda, Ramana Maharshi, Swami Vivekananda, Swami Sivananda of Rishikesh, Papa Ramdas, and other spiritual masters and teachers, as well as his own experiences, Abbot Burke illustrates the teachings of the Gita with stories which make the teachings of Krishna in the Gita vibrant and living.

What Readers say:

"This is not a book for only "Hindus" or "Christians." Anyone desiring to better their lives mentally, emotionally, and spiritually would benefit greatly by reading this book."— *Sailaja Kuruvadi*

The Upanishads for Awakening

A Practical Commentary on India's Classical Scriptures

With penetrating insight, Abbot George Burke illumines the Upanishads' practical value for spiritual seekers, and the timelessness of India's most beloved scriptures. With a unique perspective of a lifetime of study and practice of both Eastern and Western spirituality, Abbot George mines the treasures of the Upanishads and presents them in an easily intelligible fashion for those wishing to put these priceless teachings into practice

The teachings of the Upanishads are the supreme expressions of the eternal wisdom, the eternal vision of the ancient rishis (sages) of India. The truths embodied in the Upanishads and their inspired digest-summary, the Bhagavad Gita, are invaluable for all who would ascend to higher consciousness.

What Readers say:

"It is always a delight to see how he seamlessly integrates the wisdom of the West into the East." —*Roopa Subramani*

The Bhagavad Gita–The Song of God

A new translation of the most important spiritual classic which India has produced.

Often called the "Bible" of Hinduism, the Bhagavad Gita is found in households throughout India and has been translated into every major language of the world. Literally billions of copies have been handwritten and printed.

The clarity of this translation by Abbot George Burke makes for easy reading, while the rich content makes this the ideal "study" Gita. As the original Sanskrit language is so rich, often there are several accurate translations for the same word, which are noted in the text, giving the spiritual student the needed understanding of the fullness of the Gita.

For those unable to make a spiritual journey to India, a greater pilgrimage can be made by anyone anywhere in the world by simply reading The Holy Song of God, the Srimad Bhagavad Gita. It will be a holy pilgrimage of mind and spirit.

Robe of Light

An Esoteric Christian Cosmology

In *Robe of Light* Abbot George Burke explores the whys and wherefores of the mystery of creation. From the emanation of the worlds from the very Being of God, to the evolution of the souls to their ultimate destiny as perfected Sons of God, the ideal progression of creation is described. Since the rebellion of Lucifer and the fall of Adam and Eve from Paradise flawed the normal plan of evolution, a restoration was necessary. How this came about is the prime subject of this insightful study.

Moreover, what this means to aspirants for spiritual perfection is expounded, with a compelling knowledge of the scriptures and of the mystical traditions of East and West.

What Readers say:

"Having previously read several offerings from the pen of Abbot George Burke I was anticipating this work to be well written and an enjoyable read. However, Robe of Light actually exceeded my expectations. Abbot Burke explicates the subject perfectly, making a difficult and complex subject like Christian cosmology accessible to those of us who are not great theologians."—*Russ Thomas*

151

A Brief Sanskrit Glossary

A Spiritual Student's Guide to Essential Sanskrit Terms

This Sanskrit glossary contains full translations and explanations of many of the most commonly used spiritual Sanskrit terms, and will help students of the Bhagavad Gita, the Upanishads, the Yoga Sutras of Patanjali, and other Indian scriptures and philosophical works to expand their vocabularies to include the Sanskrit terms contained in them, and gain a fuller understanding in their studies.

What Readers say:

"If you are reading the writings of Swami Sivananda you will find a basketful of untranslated Sanskrit words which often have no explanation, as he assumes his readers have a background in Hindu philosophy. For writings like his, this book is invaluable, as it lists frequently used Sanskrit terms used in writings on yoga and Hindu philosophical thought.

"As the title says, this is a spiritual students' guidebook, listing not only commonly used spiritual terms, but also giving brief information about spiritual teachers and writers, both modern and ancient.

"Abbot George's collection is just long enough to give the meanings of useful terms without overwhelming the reader with an overabundance of extraneous words. This is a book that the spiritual student will use frequently."—*Simeon Davis*

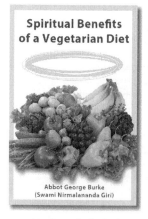

Spiritual Benefits of a Vegetarian Diet

The health benefits of a vegetarian diet are well known, as are the ethical aspects. But the spiritual advantages should be studied by anyone involved in meditation, yoga, or any type of spiritual practice.

Although diet is commonly considered a matter of physical health alone, since the Hermetic principle "as above, so below" is a fundamental truth of the cosmos, diet is a crucial aspect of emotional, intellectual, and spiritual development as well. For diet and consciousness are interrelated, and purity of diet is an effective aid to purity and clarity of consciousness.

The major thing to keep in mind when considering the subject of vegetarianism is its relevancy in relation to our explorations of consciousness. We need only ask: Does it facilitate my spiritual growth–the development and expansion of my consciousness? The answer is Yes.

A second essay, *Christian Vegetarianism*, continues with a consideration of the esoteric side of diet, the vegetarian roots of early Christianity, and an insightful exploration of vegetarianism in the Old and New Testaments.

Available as a free Kindle ebook download at Amazon.com.

Foundations of Yoga
Ten Important Principles Every Meditator Should Know

An in-depth examination of the important foundation principles of Patanjali's Yoga, Yama & Niyama.

Yama and Niyama are often called the Ten Commandments of Yoga, but they have nothing to do with the ideas of sin and virtue or good and evil as dictated by some cosmic potentate. Rather they are determined on a thoroughly practical, pragmatic basis: that which strengthens and facilitates our yoga practice should be observed and that which weakens or hinders it should be avoided.

It is not a matter of being good or bad, but of being wise or foolish. Each one of these Five Don'ts (Yama) and Five Do's (Niyama) is a supporting, liberating foundation of Yoga. An introduction to the important foundation principles of Patanjali's Yoga: Yama & Niyama

Available as a free Kindle ebook download at Amazon.com, as well as in paperback.

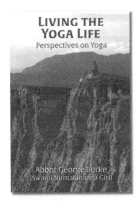

Living the Yoga Life
Perspectives on Yoga

"Dive deep; otherwise you cannot get the gems at the bottom of the ocean. You cannot pick up the gems if you only float on the surface." Sri Ramakrishna

Many people come to the joyous and liberating discovery of yoga and yoga philosophy, and then dive no deeper, resting on their first understanding of the atman, Brahman, the goal of yoga, and everything else the classic yoga philosophy teaches about "the way things are."

In *Living the Yoga Life* author Abbot George Burke shares the gems he has found from a lifetime of "diving deep." This collection of reflections and short essays addresses the key concepts of the yoga philosophy that are so easy to take for granted. Never content with the accepted cliches about yoga sadhana, the yoga life, the place of a guru, the nature of Brahman and our unity with It, Abbot George's insights on these and other facets of the yoga life will inspire, provoke, enlighten, and even entertain.

What Readers say:
"Abbot George eloquently brings the eastern practice of seeking God inwardly to western readers who have been taught to seek God outwardly."—*Bill Braddock*

May a Christian Believe in Reincarnation?

Discover the real and surprising history of reincarnation and Christianity.

A growing number of people are open to the subject of past lives, and the belief in rebirth–reincarnation, metempsychosis, or transmigration–is becoming commonplace. It often thought that belief in reincarnation and Christianity are incompatible. But is this really true? May a Christian believe in reincarnation? The answer may surprise you.

Reincarnation-also known as the transmigration of souls-is not just some exotic idea of non-Christian mysticism. Nor is it an exclusively Hindu-Buddhist teaching.

In orthodox Jewish and early Christian writings, as well as the Holy Scriptures, we find reincarnation as a fully developed belief, although today it is commonly ignored. But from the beginning it has been an integral part of Orthodox Judaism, and therefore as Orthodox Jews, Jesus and his Apostles would have believed in rebirth.

What Readers say:

"Those needing evidence that a belief in reincarnation is in accordance with teachings of the Christ need look no further: Plainly laid out and explained in an intelligent manner from one who has spent his life on a Christ-like path of renunciation and prayer/meditation."—*Christopher T. Cook*

Yoga: Science of the Absolute
A Commentary on the Yoga Sutras of Patanjali

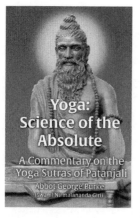

In *Yoga: Science of the Absolute*, Abbot George Burke draws on the age-long tradition regarding this essential text, including the commentaries of Vyasa and Shankara, the most highly regarded writers on Indian philosophy and practice, as well as I. K. Taimni and other authoritative commentators, and adds his own ideas based on half a century of study and practice.Serious students of yoga will find this an essential addition to their spiritual studies.

What Readers say:

"Abbot George has provided a commentary that is not only deeply informative, making brilliant connections across multiple traditions, but eminently practical. More importantly he describes how they can help one empower their own practice, their own sadhana." —Michael Sabani

The Odes of Solomon for Awakening

A Commentary on the Mystical Wisdom of the Earliest Christian Hymns and Poems

With penetrating insight, Abbot George Burke illumines the practical value of the Odes of Solomon for spiritual seekers, and the timelessness of these ancient writings. With a unique perspective of a lifetime of study and practice of both Eastern and Western spirituality, Abbot George mines the treasures of the Odes and presents them in an easily intelligible fashion for those wishing to put these priceless teachings into practice.

What Readers say:

"Both Hierodeacon Simeon's lovely translation and Abbot George's deeply insightful commentary do great justice to this most ancient and exquisite work. It will rightfully hold an honored place in any seriously spiritual library." —Brother Julian-Ozana

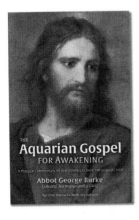

The Aquarian Gospel for Awakening, volumes 1&2

A Practical Commentary on Levi Dowling's Classic Life of Jesus Christ

In 1908 *The Aquarian Gospel of Jesus the Christ* by Levi H. Dowling appeared on the shelves of American bookstores. Immediately it evoked a response in those who intuited and sought for a deeper meaning of the person and teachings of Jesus of Nazareth. Abbot George illumines the practical value of the Aquarian Gospel for spiritual seekers, and the timelessness of this classic writing.

What Readers say:

"A perfect addition to any spiritual seeker's library, *The Aquarian Gospel for Awakening*...is a refreshingly different read about Christ's life. It is such an enjoyable book to read, I'm afraid I let my other tasks fall by the wayside - I couldn't put it down! I feel that it will enrich anyone's understanding of Jesus, no matter what your religious background is." —Mel Halloran

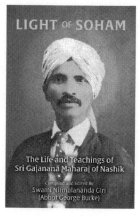

Light of Soham
The Life and Teachings of Sri Gajanana Maharaj of Nashik

At the beginning of the twentieth century, a young crippled boy in North India met a spiritual teacher in the Nath tradition of the great teachers Matsyendranath and Gorakhnath, who imparted to him the precious knowledge of yoga meditation. The boy began to apply himself to this meditation practice and became a very unusual saint indeed.

Gajanana Maharaj taught the ajapa-japa of the Soham mantra with the breath. In Light of Soham his teachings for success in Soham sadhana and spiritual life in general have been collected from the writings of himself and his disciples.

What Readers say:

"This book cuts straight to the problem of life - our separation from the Godhead - and without dwelling too much on this immediately cuts to the solution: Meditation." —Dylan Grant

Coming Soon:
The Four Gospels for Awakening
Light on the Path for Awakening

Made in the USA
Middletown, DE
30 October 2022

13768039R00102